The Powerful Entrepreneur

By: Arthur Shulsky

21st century entrepreneurial lessons told through

the greatest stories from world history.

The Powerful Entrepreneur

Arthur Shulsky

ArthurShulsky@gmail.com

Ordering Information:

Quantity sales. Special discounts are available on quantity purchases by corporations, associations, and others. For details, contact the publisher at the address above. Orders by U.S. trade bookstores and wholesalers. Please see email above.

Cover art designed by Katie Aguilar

First Edition

ISBN 978-1-979-96376-3

Visit author's website at:

www.ArthurShulsky.com

For my wife, my mother, my father and my brother

"While many powerful are referenced hereafter, there are four whom I wish to saunter above all".

Contents

People and Leadership

Planning and Structure

Production and Operations

Sales and Marketing

Bibliography

Preface

TODAY THE AVERAGE PERSON has access to more information than any of the most intellectual people of the pre-modern era. The steps taken to achieve this level of data access by the common man and woman has evolved over thousands of years, but most of this evolution has occurred in the past forty. There is a great ignorance present within our culture, and it resonates within the fabric of our own moral existence. Back no more than 100 years, the method in which data was collected and stored was more common to that of antiquity than that of today.

While human theory and ability to collect and manage information has changed vastly over the course of human history, it wasn't until the past fifteen years where the activity of every single human experience was recorded and tracked via social media. Very specific improvements over the course of the very recent past, such as the evolution of independent photojournalism and modern data warehousing, has played an extremely important role in the ability for humans to gather personal data of consistency and longevity. To be put simply, when I die there will be so much virtual data regarding my life that it will be preserved for ages in the first of a long line of stored human experiences. My father, my grandfather and all of the men and women before them must rely upon second accounts within books to tell their stories of human existence. It is a sad reality that personal human history up until the year 2000 has the highest risk of being lost to time.

Beyond personal human history comes macro level history that every society and group of people between the Neolithic period to today has had a hand in forming. Until print allowed for the mass distribution of information to the common person, history and experience was passed by word of mouth. We must never forget the importance base level human communication played in the recollections we have of the history of our ancestors. By using history to prove our foundation, humans have been basing logical thought processes on the experiences of our past brethren for an eternity. In other words, "How would my mother or father have handled this same adversity?"

While we can go on and on about how the world today is different than the world of yesterday, the world of our passed brothers and sisters is a deep history of proven actions at the expense of all human existence. This experience is relevant today at so many levels but is often misplaced due to the surface level ideologies of the current techno-culture.

After having obsessed over a plethora of business advice books and historical science literature over the past twenty years, it was apparent to me that something was missing within our realm of modern accumulated knowledge. No one takes characters outside of the 21st century and applies them to lessons within the modern era as much as they can, or should. Just because Genghis Khan had no computer does not mean his success is unwarranted in the modern age. Just because Joan of Arc used her voice and faith to turn the tide of the war with England does not mean she would not find that same success today in a world where our voices our blocked between a median of pre-determined algorithms and battery lives.

So here it is, in all of its glory, my attempt at taking many of the greatest characters from history and deriving relevant entrepreneurial theory from their life stories. These are the most legendary people in history, and still to this day they represent the extremes in our modern aspirations for power, wealth, fame and influence. To forget history is to repeat negative history, to remember history is to repeat positive history.

The Powerful Entrepreneur

One

Blood, Sweat and Numbers

LET US TAKE A STEP back in time. To a time when success was earned in blood, sweat and dirt. The world of today wasn't even a figment of a fragment of an imagination. A time so long past where murder, rape, starvation, plague and enslavement was as common as Honda's, bottled water and Twitter posts today. The era was that of endurance for humanity. The single most important component in human societal development and survival was the only focus. Our 21st century idea of necessity is infinitely pathetic compared to the needs and demands of this time. Let us talk about a time in which gods were as bountiful as Costco's and ailments as prevalent as utility bills.

5,000 years ago, was a time in which we as a people focused on one thing and one thing only; food. It was so important that children were worked to death just to feed other children. It was the entire focus of every man, woman and child on the planet. The pharaohs spent their time ensuring that the people had enough of it, had access to it and ensured that no one was going to steal it from under their bloodied fingers. Wars were fought, lives were lost, droughts rose and floods came. It was a time for honorable focuses and yet desperate actions. The ideas we hold humbling were used as barbaric instruments of fate by our ancestors.

Imagine a man at this time with a moderate level of societal responsibility. Let's just say that this person was a farmer. This farmer has access to land, water on good years and his own two hands. His family was a support mechanism which drove the machine of his endurance. His wife worked by his side to ensure optimization of daily work. The family unit was core to this society and inconsistent with our 21st century progressive ideologies. No man or woman was more important than the other, but roles within the family unit were simply mandated by the will to survive within a barbaric society. Today, any fool can walk to a store to pick up the week's wanton necessities. Back then, the family unit lived or died dependent on foundation, consistency and determination.

Business was king as always and business revolved around one thing; earning food. Feed an army, gain immense power. Feed a family, live a long life. Feed yourself, live another day.

We take for granted the ailments of our time and throw out the ailments of our human ancestors. The proven approach between modern progressive theory versus ancient traditional law is easily apparent. Our ancestors lived to a strong code of conduct to survive and proved they could do it over the generations of consistent strife.

At this time, a town of 5,000 people was a thriving place of commerce, desire and passion. The ancient Egyptians were practical at heart and focused on the archaic gluttonies of men and women. With an extra sack of grain per year, a family could ensure their spot on the local administrator's lists of influence. Power was derived from administration over other men. Administration required infrastructure, management and accounting of product and people. Men with power lived and died off of the men without. Just like today, information was power beyond power.

Every harvest or season was focused on storing, predicting, driving, organizing, combining and re-distributing the major wealth of the time. Much like our tax system today, which redistributes wealth to units in need, the Egyptians ensured their people lived to fight another year. Year after year, the food was stored and eaten. Life for our ancestors literally could be summarized into nine words, "Year after year the food was stored and eaten." Humans have lived through thousands of years of agricultural expansion because of these nine words, nine words totally forgotten today.

While individual battles were fought, won and lost on the farmer's soil, the wars were won at the local administrator's office. Earliest inventions around 'counting' were implemented in a simple form. The ability to collect and store data in a reliable and traceable form revolutionized the era. The Egyptians at this time conquered all because they were able to store and track data better than anyone else. Data management was in a barbaric form. Dashes made on bones and tied to jars or stacks. Tallies pressed into brick and stone while kept in giant rooms surrounded by brick and mud. Organization was crucial, and follies were punishable by death at the hand of a god.

The power within decision making was fundamentally based around the ability to understand the current state of the world around them, much like today. While we lived and died by the scythe, we grew and flourished by archaic accounting.

Today we live in a world where 'counting' is a minimum expectation for preschoolers to reach kindergarten. Accounting as a trade has become one in which men and women focus lifetimes studying one element of one organization of one industry before laying to retirement. We have mastered our ability to count and derive value from information and yet have subjected the entire human existence to its doctrines. Life has a funny way of teasing progress while being entirely immutable.

Two

Lead from The Front

THE YEAR WAS 1918 and the world was at war. The most brutal war for the soldier class ever to have existed and hopefully will ever have existed. Gas raids, trench foot, no man's land and relentless artillery fire was the day-to-day life of a soldier on the front lines during World War I. Many people today forget this, but America was a minor nation in the global political climate of the early 20th century. American isolationism was a very real thing, and the European powers of the day viewed America with much abhorrence.

After four grueling years of constant bloodshed, an entire generation of Western Europeans had been eliminated from the almanacs of time. I personally have visited the cemeteries in France for the fallen western soldiers who sacrificed their lives for their monarch overlords; endless fields of forgotten graves.

America was fighting a different war compared to their allies and enemies. While the German, French, English, Italian and Austro-Hungarian empires were fighting because of the monarch ruling class, the Americans were fighting for self-actualization. The Caucasian immigrants that came over during the late 19th and early 20th century to America had already escaped the monarch factions and were shipped back to Europe in order to fight a superficial war of attrition. It is to no surprise the dream that was America was fighting for its very life within those trenches, alongside the very monarchs she wished to oppose. This was ironically an army of men fighting for freedom, all while fighting for a king.

Strong leaders were needed during this time period, unlike any other period in history. Imagine the most desperate place a man can find himself, facing the inevitable march of death day in and day out. Leaders needed to be ready to fight and die for the men alongside them; fight and die they surely did. There was one decisive battle in central France in which the American forces demonstrated unparalleled valor and helped the western allies mark a major blow against the exhausted German juggernaut. The Battle of Saint-Mihiel was what history would remember it by. America was unproven and inexperienced. The German forces were on the retreat and the stronghold of Metz, France was up for grabs. The Americans made an aggressive push under General Pershing to take the stronghold and drive a decisive blow to the German defensive.

A young brilliant tank commander Colonel George Patton was in command of 144 freshly assembled French built American manned tanks, tasked with punching a hole big enough in the German line that the American infantry force could gain ground. Imagine that battlefield, imagine hell itself. Death was present as far as the eye could see. No hope existed for the common man or woman, only God for all and luck for others. Patton lead his freshly trained force from the front that day without hesitation. He took on an equal share of risk and ensured his troops maintained their moral to continue to fight and push without restraint. Patton proved himself a worthy leader and a brave man, worthy to stand within the halls of the world's greatest heroes and heroines at that moment in his life. He inspired his men around him to achieve greater strides of courage than would have been imagined.

Let us take a step forward in time and put together some 21st century logic behind the actions of our ancestors. Today's technology industry functions in a very similar light as America did during World War I. The business industry as a whole today is much like the world in 1917. The elites at the top of our food chain control the influence, and the rest of us are fighting in the trenches to make a dollar. Our political crony capitalist system functions a lot like a monarchy in that power is passed down through right of trust fund babies, and the rest of us depend on the imitation of stability resonating from the top down to support our futures.

Real estate, healthcare, insurance, banking, transportation and manufacturing all function within the guidelines of the 20th century.

While the world and the economy has been exhausted beyond hope, here comes a new face in the war without any 20th century stigma, ignorance or regulation holding it back. The online tech industry that has boomed over the past 15 years has completely redefined the nature of our workforce, how we communicate at work and in our personal lives, how money is made and how money is spent. Much like America had something to prove entering into World War I, the tech industry has a lot to prove entering into the macro-level economic system. The cliché aspect of all of this is like America in World War I, the tech industry is winning and winning strong.

Let's talk about the battlefield situation and leave the macro level landscape to the fates that design it. For the common man or woman in the tech industry waging a relentless battle for supremacy over stiff competition, unknown brands, untested business models and unclear trajectories, the achievement of success holds a strong foundation within the halls of leadership and honor. As an entrepreneur within the tech space leading a team, concept or product to victory demands a strong ability to take risk and drive home a demonstration of courage. Much like Colonel Patton leading the fight from the front with his tank regiment, you as the aspiring entrepreneur must lead from the front in order to achieve any permanent forward progress.

It also goes beyond the simple ability to just lead from the front and demonstrate courage. One must hold honor in high priority due to the very fabric of the tech industry landscape. Just because someone has 300,000 followers on twitter does not make them a tech professional or an entrepreneur at that. The tech industry and the entrepreneurial industry at its foundation is ground in the fact that true value is king above all else, and the perception of value will ultimately die fast. Approach your venture believing an honorable product offering of legitimate value will not only win you the battle but will finish the war.

Three

Quantitative Analysis at Its Best

IT IS FROM HUMBLE INTENTIONS that I write this piece about a topic that even someone of my accomplishment begets the pleasure to preach. I have spent my entire life applying quantitative logic towards everyday problems. This particular individual succeeded at this endeavor on every political, military, economic and societal level. Napoleon Bonaparte was the greatest quantitative reasoner on the face of the planet and still holds this reign today. For the longest time, my affection for the honor this man commanded among his own people was always something I held with great esteem. Our connection was quantitative reasoning and logical coordinated attacks toward problems and threats. While Napoleon used his influence to conquer and quell, I wish to use my powers to build and inspire.

Let's begin by defining quantitative reasoning. Such a simple exercise, but the theory eludes some people. If I have a problem (X) and need to obtain consequence (Y), what form of action (A) optimizes my predictable consequence based upon statistics (Q).

$$(Q > A) * X = Y$$

Quantitative reasoning.

The Emperor Napoleon wrote: "There is no man more pusillanimous than I when I am planning a campaign. I purposely exaggerate all the dangers and all the calamities that the circumstances make possible. I am in a thoroughly painful state of agitation. This does not keep me from looking quite serene in front of my entourage; I am like an unmarried girl laboring with child."

Problems exist throughout life; it is completely unavoidable. If your life exists to run from problems then you're only running into more problems. If your life revolves around answers to problems then you are able to swat them away, simple as this. Napoleon was the master at this metaphor. The man was born of a moderate wealth during a time of pure monarchs. France was so early in its grand revolution that many members of the ruling monarchy were still alive and prominent. The death of the direct monarchs was not the death of the monarchy because in a healthy monarchy lines of succession always exist, and the French were masters at lines of succession.

Let's grab a very specific example because Napoleon tackled so many problems during his reign. Most people know him as a general, when in reality, he was the master statesman. He fully reorganized the interior structure of the military and the government to great effectiveness. The administration focused entirely on population health, industry and food growth. The French people had enough culture to sustain a solid social variable no matter the changes introduced. Finally, the military allowed Napoleon to truly express his masterclass talent. While his assistance in all forms of government existed to a high standard, his presence on the battlefield was insurmountable to the day's actions.

There were so many brilliant battles fought by Napoleon; it does him little justice to describe them with such brevity. The one that sticks to mind though was in 1800 when the French and the Austrians were fighting each other over the rights to Northern Italy. Italy had been ruled over by the Austrians for almost 100 years. That's as long as our modern world was from World War I and as long as World War I was from Napoleon.

Napoleon was aggressive in his first international offensive. It was 1800, and Napoleon was sent into Northern Italy to relieve a siege versus Genoa, which the French held. Napoleon ignored the siege and conquered Milan instead, using his quantitative reasoning to predict the outcome would be a lifted siege to Genoa. Napoleon was ultimately wrong. The siege of Genoa remained in place, and the French started to lose grip over Genoa. At this moment, Napoleon decided to attack the Austrian force head-on and intercept the Austrians to start The Battle of Marengo in 1800 A.D. Napoleon, at that moment, was able to use his absolute most brilliant quantitative mind and delivered a miraculous effort on the tactical battlefield to acquire this major victory. He leveraged his decision by banking on his most prominent strength. By taking control at the macro level early, he forced his opponent to play aggressive. Napoleon countered with a beautifully superior tactical assault. Every step of the way, Napoleon saw each angle and through the use of statistics, subjection and strategic prowess had won the war and defeated the Austrian army.

Business today is no different from the aspiring efforts of Napoleon in 1800. As a business, you must conquer your own Europe and strive to achieve the impossible to earn the victory. We as entrepreneurs in the 21st century face micro and macro level problems every single day. Some are visible, and some are lurking unknown. It is without hesitation that we strive to decrease the unknown events and fend off the visible threats. Businesses are much like battlefields; you have an infinite number of subjective assessments of the surrounding environment. You try to mitigate them, but they always exist. Creatives try to capture the subjective and turn them into objective products. Technically gifted individuals attempt to remove subjective consequences by assembling specific formulas or algorithms.

If I walk into a room on a normal Tuesday during the workweek and stare at a direct problem with a team of my peers, what are the next steps? I first attempt to understand the problem at hand, followed by strategically thinking about every possible consequence due to every possible action. I label the desired conclusion and understand all of the distractions and distinct decisions that should be made to solve the problem. With the optimum theory in place, we use quantitative reasoning to verify this solution is indeed worth investing resources towards achieving. If this is not the case, then we should choose action number two and so on down the line. Quantitative reasoning used as a mandatory vetting process at internal decision making is the single greatest step a man or woman can achieve in business exercise. Fast, consistent quantitative reasoning to derive an assured victory at every corner.

Napoleon did it on the battlefield and sowed the death of many, as we in the 21st century exercise these same strengths while ensuring the continued development of our brothers and sisters.

Four

Cash as a Resource

WHAT TRULY REPRESENTS the fabric of a society? Is it music, art, science, discovery or conquest? While a conflict and an end result is never the same, the method of achieving that result is always based upon the exact same fundamental logic. Are we able to surpass this conflict and achieve a result? This question is crucial to understanding how the human mind processes the idea of available resources. Resources are the fabric of society and without infrastructure in place to ensure constant access to resources, an idea will never materialize, and an action will always fall up short. The main resource we take for granted today, which drove our ancestors into the ground, is food. For businesses and ventures, people play a hand as the ultimate resource. For many different organizations around the world, resources come in many different shapes and sizes. How we view resources, and how we drive our actions by those views, is what defines our humanity in many ways.

There is no better example when discussing resource management and how resources drive our actions to the ultimate end than when we discuss the Achilles heel of Adolf Hitler during World War II. Hitler was a juggernaut of a man fueled by his lunacy, lust for power and willingness to break the rules to get there. His selfish, gluttonous and aggressive actions at the risk of the men and women around him was synonymous with the ultimate fate of the Third Reich. In 1940, the German empire had the largest and most powerful military this world had ever seen; military infrastructure that makes the 21st century U.S. military look like kids with just really cool toys. This army was millions strong and supported by the most dominant war machine ever built, being the panzer and the panzer grenadier companies.

Hitler knew exactly what resource was going to lose him the war before the war ever even started. He labeled the issue at the onset of his early campaigns and knew that every step needed to be taken to remove the Achilles heel from the equation. The German empire needed oil, grain and coal in heavy supplies in order to fuel the military companies under Hitler's control. Hitler's insanity and hatred towards other races guided his feet, but Hitler's need for necessary resources is what guided his hands.

Before Operation Barbarossa, Hitler and Russia were allies, and Germany was heavily dependent on Russian Oil imports to fuel its immense mechanized military and supporting industry. Hitler was unable to accept this as his limitation and decided to tap into the German national oil reserves to mount Operation Barbarossa in June of 1941. The operation was a major success, and the German army almost accomplished their task of completely invading Moscow. Panzer grenadier companies were mounted German infantry rifle and machinegun units utilizing armored half-tracks for mobile capability. As you can imagine, there is nothing more terrifying than a Nazi panzer grenadier platoon driving upon your position full-force. The Russians were completely taken off-guard and their professional army destroyed. Stalin decided to implement his own aggressive military campaign to counter Hitler and forced his population to adhere to a strict conscription doctrine or perish.

Let's imagine for a second how much gasoline a World War II Panzer IV tank needed in order to function. It was a heavy amount of fuel, and there was no getting around the fact that a powered down tank is just as useful as a destroyed tank. The machinery is what gave the Germans the power to conquer the Russians and yet, oil was why the Germans failed to conquer the Russians. It hit a point where the German military needed to desperately change its strategy once the Russians were able to mount a counter attack. Long story short, a Blitzkrieg is useless without the blitz! As soon as the Germans were forced to fight a long infantry war with a Russian peasant army in the middle of the winter, Hitler heard his death music. One final effort by the Germans, called the Battle of

Kiev, was the German last-ditch effort to kill the Russian beast. Oil was out of grasp from Germany, and Hitler's grand plan was crushed before it could "truly" ever begin. We like to think about the horrors of World War II as an ultimate, but nothing emerges as comparable if Hitler would have had enough of the crucial resource, oil, to have won.

Nothing makes me realize how far we have come as a global population than when I think about the Eastern front during World War II. Businesses today fight hard to survive every day, but rarely do we compare the effort to the hardship of our ancestors whom have overcome far greater adversity. The beauty that is the 21st century should inspire us to fully utilize the positive opportunities in front of our doorsteps in honor of the sacrifices made by our ancestors.

As a small, large or solo business owner, we must study and understand the mistakes of our forefathers to grow our own standing in this competitive world. Hitler's story demonstrates the duality of our fate and how are dependency on God-granted resources guides and shapes our character. Cash for a business in the 21st century is the food of the Egyptians, it is the oil of Hitler and it is the oxygen of our kids. Without cash you stop, with cash you move and earning cash means earning that win. It is so easy to make these bold claims without anything backing up the talk. Every day in this world, we hear and see money as the means to an end without any clear path to get there. The standard variable, though, is in the 21st century, cash is always an element of that journey.

The story about Operation Barbarossa and the ultimate defeat of Hitler represents our entrepreneurial society's Achilles heel. To make overly risky decisions because of an uncontrollable dependence on a resource is to predict the outcome of the war. We must analyze how we, as business owners, explain our internal understanding of cash in our lives. If it indirectly guides your actions and you are able to achieve the need without exposing your logical decision making, then I promise you have now achieved the first step towards winning the longest war you will ever fight; life.

Five

Debt as a Resource

DEBT DESERVES A LONG conversation and a good story. This is one of my personal favorite tales, mostly because this single moment shaped the entire world almost more than any other single action in history. The story has to do with debt and the indebtedness we allow ourselves to embrace. It deals with how we as a human society can experience over-reliance on a third party to fuel our needs and desires.

Debt comes in many different shapes and sizes, whether it be debt to friend for an action or debt to a bank for money. While cash drives the "figurative" world, debt in its most general form drives the "literal" world.

Let's take a step back in time to a period not unlike our own. The world was civilized, men and women were objectified all while barbaric desires overtook practical necessities. The world was in the 4th century and the place was central Europe. The Roman Empire was still at its peak of global dominance but held its status with a sense of blissful ignorance. That was the Roman Empire. The entire known world was subject to Roman influence, and only one culture truly ever escaped the Roman doctrines. The Central German barbaric tribes still held close to their original beliefs. The Romans were never able to conquer the endless tribes of gothic pagans.

What we can't have, we want only more of.

The 4th century Romans were self-indulgent gluttons with little resemblance to the proud heritage that true Roman men and women adhered to with such envy during Julius Caesar's time. Romans had acquired a sense of immunity to the ailments of the age due to their centuries-old power structure that was slowly becoming harder and harder to maintain in the changing world. One of the major setbacks of this time period was the lack of Roman participation within the legions protecting Rome from the rest of the world. Roman born men had become unwilling or not needing to participate in the military, and instead, focused on more bureaucratic trades. The era of Old Rome was long gone, and the current Romans were more worried about their personal aspirations than that of their crumbling empire.

Due to Roman citizens being less and less likely to physically participate in the military, the heads of government decided to increase the reliance upon third party mercenaries to protect the Roman lands. The empire had indebted itself to the reliance on gothic barbarians for their internal security from the very same barbarians, which sought to destroy Rome. There was a number of conflicts between Roman and gothic groups between the 4th and 7th century. One specific encounter that stands out was the incursion into Thrace, which was fueled by the local Roman population fighting with the foreign gothic groups paid to protect them.

The resulting situation caused a domino effect that allowed the goths to resupply and swell their ranks of men after every village sacked. There were so many goths in the region that the Romans had caused their own snowballing doom. In 378, a great battle was fought to stop the increasingly threatening gothic warband. The battle went poorly for the Romans, and the empire suffered one of its single greatest defeats in that moment. The gothic host was free to march on the capital of Constantinople but was only slightly prevented from conquering the city. The resulting years saw massive devastation to the Roman interior, which had never been seen before.

The other major ramification that came about because of this turn-of-events was the overall distrust of the gothic people by the Romans. Barbarians from all across the empire were put to death, and this saw the end of the interior stability of Rome. The number of goths who had been brought into the empire were such a force at this point, the Roman people had no place to go to avoid them and no way to stop them. The reliance upon the gothic tribes to fill the ranks of the Roman army during these years of high military demand was simply too much for the Roman Empire to handle well. The resulting couple of centuries saw the total collapse of the Ancient Roman Empire.

Do barbarians and romans really have anything to do with modern 21st century business? I believe the lesson learned from the Roman dependence on external assistance to maintain a level of superiority over the world ensured the very downfall of the empire itself. This is so resembling of how many businesses today take on debt where debt should be avoided. Like we said before, debt takes on many different forms. Debt can be a loan from a bank, credit card, profit or revenue sharing agreement, convertible notes and even favors to peers. How we spend our time relying upon others without taking the necessary cautious steps to watch our own sustainable models is a very common way businesses in this modern world of high-tech end up failing.

A great story from my personal experience was a client of mine who received a cash offer from an investor where in return they would receive an equity standing within the company and a portion of gross revenue every quarter. My client assumed that making revenue would result in enough money to pay for the investor and pay for their own business expenses. The resulting scenario played out eventually to where our cost of sales was so high due to our extravagant paid marketing costs that we were completely unable to pay for the investor revenue split. The investor ended up receiving a clear majority of the money he had invested back into the company, and by the time the cash had dissipated, we were sitting with less equity and less money than before we had ever engaged the investor.

In summary, ensuring caution while taking on debt within the context of your business model needs to be the number one priority before any agreements or maneuvers are performed. A solid long- and short-term plan to repay the debt needs to be established early on, and gaps within the logic need to be filled before any movement can be made. Just because someone wants to give you money does not meant this person knows what your company needs or has your company's best interests at heart. Remember what the gothic barbarians did to Rome, and you will know the power many investors hold over their assets.

Six

Sustainable Revenue

THERE IS A STORY that is rarely told and even less known. It is the story about positioning. Positioning oneself into a place for success, and placing focus on the actions necessary to achieve that success. Both are equally as important as the other, and no other story in history is better representative of this thought process than the aspirations of King Fredrick II of The Holy Roman Empire in the 13th century.

To tell the story of King Fredrick is to start by explaining where the world was at this point. The Crusades had been waging for centuries, and generations on top of generations of kings, princes, soldiers, wives and children from England to Persia had been feeling the consequences of such a taxing global war. Both sides of the equation were guilty of mass atrocities at this point in our story, and neither side appeared to be relenting in their hold over prejudice and ideologies. The world was diverse and very segregated with not much having changed due to archaic methods of travel and general xenophobia. Life was a daily war for survival against countless odds, and three of the major civilizations in the world had spent centuries focusing their efforts on bloodshed and conquering.

After the Third Crusade, spending centralized resources on building another crusade was predominately used as a weapon by the church to keep the political infrastructure of the Holy Roman Empire in check. Almost a millennium after Constantine brought Christianity to the Romans, the Christian lifestyle had become more than just spiritual growth. It wasn't that Christian ideologies were a prominence within every fabric of society, but rather that every fabric of society adhered to a humanized doctrine of a Christian theocracy. In other words, Christian theocracy was the only thing holding together the Roman Empire from internal and external strife, and without this power of unification in the mix, there would be no continental governance to keep in check the powers at play. At this time in the history of the world without religious focus, the world would have destroyed itself because of the barbaric desires of men and women.

As a baby, King Fredrick II achieved the crown of Sicily after his father had passed away. Fredrick was the rightful heir to the throne of the entire Holy Roman Empire at the time. He had many men contest his place as the rightful heir, and therefore wasn't able to make a maneuver to achieve his crown until he was old enough to fight for it. After the death of his mother, Pope Innocent III became Fredrick's guardian. At a very early age, Fredrick was around the necessary resources to achieve his crown and to become a truly powerful emperor. He was an icon of his time to the highest degree. It wasn't until 1212 that Fredrick had finally won his rightful crown from the clutches of his German rivals. Once he was crowned Emperor, it became a constant pressure by the Catholic Church to lead another crusade to take Jerusalem.

With every decision Fredrick made, every place he went and every bureaucrat he interchanged with, the crusades became his most pressured task to undertake. His reign and standing within the empire was completely interlocked with the demand for him to undertake a 5th crusade. In his first attempt, he sent the Duke of Bavaria in his place in order to commence the 5th crusade, which was an ultimate failure. The church was heavily displeased at this action, and the pressure to follow through on his vows increased tremendously. Eventually, he had decided to start the 6th crusade but failed to complete the journey via the Mediterranean due to illness. This heavily displeased the church hierarchs even more, and they were left with no choice but to excommunicate Emperor Fredrick.

As you can imagine being excommunicated in the 13th century was a good way of losing any right to power that you once had. It is comparable today to getting fired from a job, having the IRS freeze your assets, losing your mortgage and getting sued by your own brother. It was a fast road to the poorhouse, and Fredrick had no intention of letting his train stop running. Therefore, he commenced on the 6th crusade while being excommunicated and without having the support of the church to do so. While Fredrick's actions were honorable at this time, the infrastructure needed to achieve those intentions was heavily limited.

In 1229, the unthinkable happened with the signing of a truce between Al-Kamil, the Sultan of Egypt, and Emperor Fredrick II. The city of Jerusalem was handed over to the Christians, and for the first time since the city was taken by the legendary Saladin, a Christian mass was held within the city. As part of the treaty, the city was not allowed to hold a defensive garrison and therefore sat undefended in a sea of enemy's. The goal was fully achieved but had no sustainable model to allow for the success to be experienced. Also, by taking the city and the crown for himself while excommunicated, ensured that Fredrick received no support from Europe or the church. Fredrick won the battle, achieved his mission and yet exposed his success to a losing fate. The city was taken by force shortly thereafter, and the city of Jerusalem wasn't freed from Islamic rule by the British Empire for another 700 years.

Fredrick's journey to achieve his most prominent goal was one of success and completion. He achieved the exact task he was destined to achieve, yet there was little in the way of foundation built around that success for it to flourish into a beneficial victory. This story is a good representation of the hundreds of thousands of businesses that have been started by hungry determined entrepreneurs. With the right determination, any entrepreneur can experience the ultimate win and create his or her own business venture.

It is a great day indeed when we are able to receive that notice from the state that our corporation or partnership has been created. It is a day to celebrate when we finish a product or project that will set our business apart from the crowd. There is little to do but rejoice when that first contract is signed with a powerful client. All of these achievements embody the same status in our thoughts and dreams as the city of Jerusalem was to Fredrick.

I can't count how many times I have heard success stories from people before the real achievement ever began. Pride is the true downfall of the victors, and pride inhibits the ability for a person to properly plan and sustain the infrastructure for prolonged success in today's world. The minute you believe a win has set the road in front of you is the exact minute the ground falls from beneath your feet. Victories are only sustainable if a model has been developed to leverage the standing achieved after the fact. We are a product of a collection of actions, and no single action can derive our future standing. Like most failed start-ups, Fredrick believed his quest was greater than the infrastructure it should have been built around. Build a sustainable revenue model first, then build the business around that model.

Seven

The Weight of an Idea

WHAT TRULY DEFINES the nature of our story? In my long experience of appreciating the older generations, age confers a wisdom youthful spirit cannot understand. We can logically understand death, but we are unable to look death in the face. Once death resides in our soul, we as humans finally learn the wisdom garnered by old age. Some of us are privy to this knowledge, while others walk blindly down the path of eventual awakening. Hopefully the smoke comes before the fire.

There was a gentleman that wrote dark unending stories during America's emergence as a small, unproven nation with the world in its way. Edgar Allen Poe as a literary contributor to the culture of this nation is so profound that my sole mentioning of his name within my own pitiful writing is engrained in humility and affection. Little is there to write that has not already been written regarding his contributions, and I believe it important to note this article does not necessarily encompass his writing directly. Edgar Allen Poe, besides being a demigod of American literature, is notorious for another reason.

If you've ever read his work, you will understand one unending theme present within all of his well-known work. The theme is hopeless desperation and the morbid fragility that is the human character. To be the man to have had such an influence over so many generations and all held within a basis of constant poetic doom took no average life to obtain. Poe had to sacrifice his entire life's sense of visceral happiness, even if that sacrifice came unwillingly. In order for him to obtain an absolute mastery over the internal strife of man, Poe had to embody that strife outside, inside and beyond all doubt.

There is no better example of this "need to embody" theory than Edgar Allen Poe. It is my belief that this sad fate of his would be a point of discontent in his life, even when taking into considerations his contributions. But at the time, even this luxury was something he had to forego in order to obtain the level of mastery his art form required. With little doubt the most demonstrative aspect of Poe's burden resonated with the sheer lack of acceptance his work carried during his direct life. Poe had little in terms of monetary gains or influence to show for his writing career. His professional shortfalls only aided his sense of disparity towards his own life, and it wasn't until only a few years before his death he had received any meaningful accreditation.

When Poe died, a rival of his wrote a horribly slanderous obituary with the attempt to enact revenge for the strife Poe had caused him. The opposite effect happened, and Edgar Allen Poe was catapulted into the history books as one of the most legendary Americans to have ever existed. The irony of Poe's story was he received so much success after his death only because he was able to leverage the very desperation of his own life's shortcomings in order to achieve that success. Edgar Allen Poe still to this day represents the very essence of what we aspire to become and it requires our life's complete sacrifice to obtain that aspiration.

Not much has changed since the coming of the new millennium. The very concept of mastery over one's aspirations comes at the sacrifice of an entire life's worth of potential. The modern world of business and technology is a true demonstrative setting for this theory of "need to embody". Our most successful and brilliant entrepreneurs had to undertake the very fabric of their setting to obtain any ground against hostile competitors. Steve Jobs, Bill Gates, Mark Zuckerberg, Elon Musk and other well-known innovators needed to go above and beyond the sheer invention of "good ideas" to obtain a mastery at their chosen fields. It is with little conflict that we associate success with sacrifice, in fact it is one of the most American ideas that have come out of the modern age.

Let's get back to the nature of you as an entrepreneur in this age of highly competitive and unstable industry positions. Brand loyalty, to an extent, is dead, the ability to hold an idea over the heads of competitors has almost completely diminished due to social media, and the financial strain necessary to become an entrepreneur is beyond challenging today. These obstacles require dramatic sacrifice to be overcome.

I have a great personal story about a group of entrepreneurs with literally every opportunity at their fingertips: youth, elite education and most importantly, money. It is without a doubt that this group of individuals is by far my least impressive client and my biggest headache to administer consulting services to. The reason for their total lack of success is due entirely to their lack of sacrifice. They have sacrificed no pride in order to build their company to their image. They cherish the opinions of others with the lowest of denominators, and months will pass, followed by millions of dollars in capital all to prove a point masked by pride.

Sacrifice takes on an infinite number of forms for us men and women. Its disguises number the same as our inhibitions, desires and needs. The ability to label the areas of most sacrifice in order to achieve mastery over one's aspirations is mandatory to the success story yet to be written.

If I need to bring this example around to my own knowledge of sacrifice, I had to make a very difficult decision in 2014 I would never regret. The decision to leave a six-figure job for the whisper of an idea that I had was unprecedented in my life. Without this sacrifice, I never would have been able to start my consulting firm, administer to my large client base, develop my own software and write this very book you are reading today.

Eight

Innovation and Competition

IT IS ONE OF THE EASIEST claims to make after the fact: striking it rich with luck and staking a claim on a chosen mastery once the bloodsuckers come panhandling. All of the great cliché business quotes come from men and women falling face first into a pool of gold because of pre-position. The 21st century is completely saturated with the barrel-chested entrepreneur, financier or innovator falling into place, rather than climbing to that place.

We will take a step back to a simpler time in American history when any person willing could potentially strike it rich without much in terms of tactful pursuit of a chosen mastery. The 1849 California Gold Rush saw the dawn of a new age of American growth and dominance. The Gold Rush is credited to having been the fuel to start the California fire that still burns today. Oil, transportation, agriculture, shipping and modern technology all owe homage to the 1849 Gold Rush. The macro-economic positives are easy to label, and yet most textbooks don't teach us about how lessons from the Gold Rush micro-economy still resonate within many major industries of the 21st century.

The Gold Rush. We usually picture the typical image of an old prospector fishing through a river with a rusty old pan searching for those precious nuggets. These images aren't far off at all when it comes to the earliest of gold mining pioneers. Rocks of gold could be found lying directly in a river or mixed in with pebbles on the bottom of a ravine. This quick money is what was marketed to the masses to flock the west in search of instant wealth; the new new world.

As more and more competitors got into the mix over time, the old styles of harvesting gold became slowly obsolete, and what was competitive before was now a disadvantage. Groups of gold rushers continued to collaborate more and more, leading to the innovations of how gold mining was conducted. Larger and more mechanical methods of dredging, combing and scooping earth were designed to increase the output previously unexperienced. As these methods became more common, the average joe "49er" couldn't compete solo. The pressure to join into laboring groups fueled by machinery and automation further ensured the economic landscape of the Gold Rush was changing every day.

Eventually the cost to participate in the Gold Rush directly was on par with the reward for taking the risk. Since large organizations had innovated to such a high degree, the landscape for competition between companies became the micro-environment. The definition of competition for the average worker changed completely, and spending time ensuring his or her association with a top producing organization rather than directly searching for gold became the day-to-day goal. To pay for transportation costs, housing, food, medical issues and family costs became so inundated within the society being built around the gold mining industry, the average person worked daily to sustain his or her ability to work daily. The dream that was had become the reality that is.

The Gold Rush in California is one of the best examples of how the competitive landscape can change given enough time. The Gold Rush changed so quickly that the study of this competitive theory is easily expressed with correlating actions and results. The invention of a new machine and the growing groups of workers ensured the landscape developed into an efficient producer. The competition eventually catches up if there is enough reward to do so, and this process continues until the resource is gone. The market for the resource dissipates, or the barriers to entry become so great that competition stops from the ground up.

Taking this knowledge from our understanding of how competitive environments evolve over time we can place this same theory into the functional happenings present within many industries of the 21st century. Specifically, the financial services markets for the public company sector today. The need for oversight, analysis, execution and consistency for large public companies today is at an unprecedented scale. If we take a walk back in time when the public company sector was still an emerging capitalist idea, any skilled person could walk into the industry and obtain wealth built upon self-reliance and determination. Today, this fact is non-existent in our prolific public financial services industry. Only the largest organizations with the most resources can compete for the billions of dollars available to them. One would think with such a large resource pull to invest with, public companies would cast a broad net to satisfy their demands of financial application and compliance. In reality, the large pool of funds is mostly targeted to very large and distinct organizations with broad focus rather than niche focus.

The Gold Rush economy is very much representative of the competitive landscape of wall street today. Very few make a lot of money, while the rest of the employee workforce earns to survive another day at the office. Innovation within the financial services industry has dismembered the power of the solo player. Speed of trading, speed of reaction and the intercommunication between the largest organizations ensures the common man and woman must invest his or her time into driving an image of apparent value towards the company directly, rather than investing 100% of time into the task itself. The non-productive focus required to stay relevant within the massive organizations that dominate the public financial services sector has become the quintessential definition of what survival looks like for this industry.

To take this back to the general entrepreneur, we must fully understand the status of the industry we plan to enter. Understanding your target market and how your competition is innovating to engage your target market is the most crucial component of building a sustainable business. Men and women playing their hands within a technically saturated and human saturated market must play into the hands of the largest companies. These men and women are not entrepreneurs by definition and will need to spend their time constantly re-evaluating their own usefulness to their corporate overseers, on top of actually completing the job. The aspiring entrepreneur who takes the steps necessary to understand the status of the competitive landscape will ensure they are taking the proper steps towards leading from the innovative front.

Nine

Prosperity Leads to Restraint

ONE OF MY MOST CHERISHED historical research projects has been my study of eastern history. The history of the far east is by far the greatest wealth of historical context ripe for analysis due to its longevity and consistency. The history of China is one of immense honor to study for many reasons. One reason that correlates with this story is China's unending struggle for self-control and constant drastic changes in ruling power the culture has experienced for many millennia. While the power structure may change, the country and the people themselves have always and will always continue to flourish. It is with this great singular variable of cultural survival that gives China the nickname "King of Historical Study" in my book.

There were many times in Chinese history when the actions taken could be described as some of the worst atrocities in the history of mankind. There are also many more examples of when China was the rock our entire world depended on for innovation, growth and advancement. This story is one of the later and represents the position and actions of many entrepreneurs today in so many ways.

The Sui Dynasty has a very important role throughout the lifespan of China. Since it was a pivotal moment in so many innovative ways, the time period stands out as one of the best throughout all of Chinese history. When Emperor Wen conquered the southern half of China, he had cemented his name and the Sui Dynasty into the history books. His conquest and unification of mainland China brought the nation and its people into a golden age of agriculture, growth, innovation and new orders. Emperor Wen eventually passed the dynasty over to his son Emperor Yang, and this event would cause ripples within the fabric of Chinese history forever.

Emperor Yang inherited an empire of unparalleled wealth and prosperity of the likes that hadn't been seen for many generations. The opportunity awaiting Emperor Yang and the people of China was without equal. This opportunity was reaped and utilized by the young emperor. Now, utilization has many forms, and all across our planet people utilize resources at their disposal in a plethora of ways. In this instance, Emperor Yang believed he was going to have the opportunity to accomplish many great things. Therefore, he utilized his resources with such a mindset.

To start this tremendous journey, we will discuss his expansion wars into Vietnam. One of his most successful accomplishments as emperor was his conquest of Vietnam early in his reign. He had sent expeditions into Vietnam in order to re-occupy the territory. His forces faced stiff opposition, including war elephants, but were eventually successful in taking back control of the Vietnam province. This ended many failed attempts by his father to accomplish this same task. While the military campaign was an ultimate success, reward was short lived due to malaria and other tropical illnesses throughout the occupation force.

Alongside his early military actions, Emperor Yang spent an enormous amount of national wealth, manpower and resources in the construction of the Grand Canal, which linked northern and southern China. This canal still remains in use today and is also the longest canal ever built. This tremendous task costed a tremendous number of resources, and the conscription requirements necessary to do the job drained the people of China.

On top of this great infrastructure achievement, the emperor decided to restore The Great Wall. This venture was at such a high cost to the people of China that the very stability of the nation came into question. Rebellion became a very direct threat, and the level of conscription and resource requirements necessary to complete the task was offset by the losses spurred by rebellion and revolt.

Finally, after the successful military conquest in Vietnam and the completion of the canal, Emperor Yang amassed a truly terrifying army in Northern China to conquer Korea. This army was millions strong and was an exceptional sight to behold. The effort and energy that went into this initiative was without equal. The war was to no degree a success, and resources continued to pour into the campaign. At this last action by Emperor Yang, the people of China eventually led a great rebellion against the Sui Dynasty. With the military power of the Sui destroyed, it was only a matter of time before rebel armies slowly took control of the provinces.

Emperor Yang fled the capital in the north, only to be assassinated by his own. The succession of the Sui Dynasty was also dismantled by the rebel factions, which led to the total annihilation of the Sui Dynasty. What remains of the Sui Dynasty in the Grand Canal, is a reminder to us today of what the hubris of man truly looks like.

There have been a number of times in my career working with men and women within the entrepreneurial space falling to hubris, instead of falling to restraint. There was the energetic tech founder who received funding before he had an element of a concrete plan. There was the graphic designer that landed a large client and spent her new revenue stream as if this was her new normal. There was the group of founders who by definition "hit it big" and thought private jets were a staple for trips across state. There was the app developer who got his big chance at building out a team and forgot to put budget ceilings into the contracts.

These stories go far beyond my personal experience. Every day an entrepreneur is making an investment decision, whether small or large, and in turn paving the road ahead before his feet can catch up. That road will either end off a cliff or will end onto solid ground. The majority of entrepreneurs walk off the cliff, and most of the time it's because they never saw the horizon until it was too late.

Properly budgeting for a long-term goal is the best counter to our hubris. Adhering to our strict budget and monitoring our actions is the single best way to ensure our road continues to move in the desired direction. Understand our time and money are equal investments, and investing time into tasks can ultimately out maneuver our capital investments to a high degree of ultimate collapse. As an entrepreneur, as a founder and as a freelancer, your minimalist lifestyle will help to ensure your venture never fails because of your own hubris. What is the point of constructing a Grand Canal or conducting the largest land invasion known to humanity if the support structure around you burns to the ground due to your aspiration?

Ten

The Margin and The Risk

GEORGE S. PATTON—the fortunate thing for us was this man was placed in the right place and at the right time. Unfortunately, he lived to see the death of his own kind.

There was a year back or so when I was at the local book store, and I saw a giant picture of George S. Patton on the cover of a 50%-off book. The book was written by everyone's least favorite ex-Fox News correspondent; his name is an abomination to hold within the context of any literature around George S. Patton. This objectification of Patton was deeply upsetting and was one of the reasons this chapter was written. Patton was the embodiment of the man whose human qualities have been beaten down and eliminated from the design of our society since the end of World War II.

Once war and politics became one and the same, it was clear that the honorable Patton represented the last of the men who saw humanity survive since the very beginning of human history. The media personalities and the bureaucratic politicians of the day became our new "honorable men". General George S. Patton, the last of his non-political breed, had beaten the Third Reich and was destroyed by the new definition of "honorable men".

Patton existed during a time when slavery and genocide were functional components of the enemy. Barbarism to the greatest extent, while wearing the uniform of the modern world. The fascist Nazi empire was the subjection and dismemberment of everything we hold for granted today. The German war machine was a monster the world had never seen before. Once the United

States got involved in the war, the hope for the Third Reich faltered, but the stern resolve of the Nazi party held the empire together. Fortress Europe was the nickname coined for the German defense of Europe, and it was this obstacle Patton, Montgomery, Eisenhower, Alexander, Bradley and millions of other men fought to subside.

There is a great single moment during the early stages of World War II that gives us a look into the minds of the men who held the gun pointed at Hitler. The allied invasion of Sicily in 1943 began at a time when the U.S. could barely even say they had been involved in the war yet. In North Africa, American troops had been consistently put to shame and embarrassed by German Field Marshal Erwin Rommel. British Field Marshal Bernard Montgomery held much dissatisfaction towards the fighting prowess of the American GI. To Montgomery, the American host was more of a distraction than an actual threat to the German war machine. Montgomery ensured his place at the forefront of the Sicilian invasion when the American's had demonstrated their low standing on the slight margin of victory.

In order to invade Sicily, allied forces landed in the south of the island with the intent to take Messina, which would support a mainland invasion of Italy. Montgomery had decided and convinced Generals Alexander and Eisenhower to lead the direct eastern attack. This move was easily the most conservative, most secure and had the highest chance of capturing Messina. The distance was the shortest, it had the best roads, there were less mountains and ultimately, it was more easily supported by allied naval presence. Montgomery took the conservative route because he played the game by the margins and didn't let over-zealous ideas cloud his judgement. Patton was left with the responsibility to watch Montgomery's left flank in a defensive pattern with no personal glory in sight.

Patton was not at all pleased with this underhanded display of disrespect. He immediately set off to prove the American fighting spirit was something to be feared. His most promising option was to take the path of most inconvenience and highest risk. He maneuvered the U.S. Seventh Army into an aggressive stance to take enemy positions fast and to not allow for enemy consolidation. His army fought through the most rugged terrain at a speed unprecedented at this point in the war. Patton took to the east and then brought the army around the inland to take Messina before Montgomery. The more conservative and more direct method of advancement ultimately failed to the riskier indirect approach. Patton was a hero and the American military giant was born anew.

In previous chapters, we discussed how in business we must ensure we are making wise, calculated and executable decisions with results of positive longevity. These previous chapters make up most of the groundwork when it comes to making wise and favorable decisions within the course of your business. Though, there is a very important component that is not discussed when trying to determine safe courses of action. This is called risk, and taking well thought out risks is the only way to ensure optimization of one's actions. There is a heavily subjective balance between taking risk without insight into unnecessary exposure and conducting your actions based upon a fear of risk. The later example of entrepreneur will most likely never achieve higher aspirations. The unnecessary risk taker most likely will not experience a sustainable achievement. The right balance is crucial to a business's chances to succeed over time.

Patton teaches us when intuition and professional mastery makes itself known to take a riskier course than was originally decided, there is nothing stopping us from taking the initiative to achieve our goals if pursued appropriately. We must always look to our business venture with a sense of needed urgency, only to the extent that we are covering our bases and adhering to our risk threshold. After the foundation is secured, we can and should take the risk with an aggressive pace.

Montgomery took the conservative, direct approach and wanted to ensure victory for his own glory. This left Patton and the Americans with an inglorious job of protecting the left flank and letting the English take the comfortable approach to victory. Patton was not happy, and he took a well calculated and riskier approach at victory to beat out Montgomery. He fought the indirect route to Messina via the west and won while Montgomery was bogged down taking the direct route. Calculation, risk taking and situational awareness all lead to victory over conservative, safe and assured.

Eleven

Embrace Your Weakness

THERE COMES A TIME when the fight becomes so brutal and so draining for all successful entrepreneurs that a key choice for continued prosperity rests in the hands of your ability to label a core weakness. The modern image of success is fraught with the ignorance behind the inevitable weaknesses all individuals inherently possess. It is not a matter of what the weakness is but rather when you will discover that weakness and admit its potency. The task of establishing a counter attack towards your embodied weakness is one of the single greatest achievements you as an entrepreneur can obtain.

There is an event in this world's history that can be described as a turning point for the modern world to have immerged. It caused the death of the political monarchy, the end to colonialism, the liberation of the middle east and the global emergence of the greatest nation of people.

This time period was 1914-1918 in Europe, and it engulfed the world into a war of the likes that had never been seen. World War I was the most terrifying war to have ever been fought up until this point in history. The experience of the common soldier was something no man or woman should ever have to endure. Imagine being in the boots of a man in the trenches or a woman on the frontlines. Spend two, three, four... months in a pit 5 feet deep, to stand to 6 feet tall would result in being shot by any number of lethal enemies. Trench foot was painful, socks were never dry, food was bad and threat of artillery shells during the night and attacks during the day relentless. And let's not mention, gas weapons.

Two months into the trench and the whistle blows. It is time to charge the enemy line, you are stiffer than a two by four and rusty to the point of static fear. You know the next whistle will be your turn to leave this disparate home. The whistle sounds and you lunge out of the front of the trench and take a look down the line to your left and right. Thousands of your fellow countrymen carry your weight and suspend you in a field of hallowed awe. The glory lasts but a moment until the sight of your inevitable destination sinks home. A field 500 meters long with nothing but carnage leading into the endless lines of enemy positions. Artillery shell, "Bang!" Machine Gun, "spat spat spat!" Time stops its existence; your life stops and you are a forgotten casualty of a forgotten war.

The hopeless nature of trench warfare, machine gun innovation, mass produced small arms and artillery dependent macro-strategies forced a tough reality upon the French, English and German Western forces. Something was going to work, something had to work. All sides wanted to finish this war, and the standard forces of Napoleonic era warfare were becoming obsolete right in front of the monarch's eyes. Artillery and Infantry must be supported by speed and effective power. Horse cavalry provided this level of reactionary and proactive power since the dawn of the era of man and woman. Horses are of little use in front of a machine gun and suffer from the same downsides as infantry when it comes to supportive fire from artillery and snipers. Unfortunately, a horse is unable to lay in a trench and artillery had become so effective at the later stages of the war that it was the most feared peace on the chess board. This fast demise of the cavalry was the case until the innovation and demonstration of the future of warfare.

Around 1915, the idea of the armored "landship" was already being developed by the Royal Navy of the British Empire. The British were the first movers on the development of the armored tank, way before the French and German military had bought in on the deal. The English had gone all in on tank development early in the war and started incorporating their experimentation onto the field of battle by 1916. The French at first were skeptical of the tanks resourcefulness due to inherent issues easily overcome by a simple adjustment of the enemy or poor weather. The conditions inside these early tanks were beyond unbearable due to exposed fumes, burning fuel and the heavy cylinder engines sitting open in the middle of many if these early tank models.

The French at first were heavily cautious in investing already scarce resources into the production of untested military technology. The war had at this point advanced the need for rail, aviation and small arms manufacturing to burden the French. The usefulness of the tank became very apparent after British field success, and by 1917, the French took on the task of developing the single most effective version of the tank for this era. French industrialism was the pride of the entire war, and eventually the French developed and built over 3,000 Renault FT's by the time the war had ended. The Renault FT was such a strong player on the battlefields of World War I, the tank lasted over three decades until World War II technology far surpassed its resourcefulness.

The Germans, on the other hand, were very late into the tank development game by the time the English and the French were on full scale manufacturing of the mechanical beasts. Germans were not only skeptical of the tank, but were also stubborn to a point. Their slow reaction towards proprietary tank development is easily represented by the mere 20 German A7V's built during the war. The Germans were industrially stretched to the limit fighting a war against three major powerhouses in the west and a sleeping beast in the far west. German naval technology was the workhorse of the war and could be attributed with one of Germany's greatest strengths during the Great War. Submarines were a large percentage of German heavy manufacturing output.

German top brass saw this unapparent yet potent weakness and went to work devising a strategy to make an initiative to address the issue of under-developed tank technology. While Germany had the power to innovate, build and develop tanks, the timing issues with the ongoing war were very apparent. Germans invested resources into developing the counter to the tank; the armor piercing bullet. Once the armor piercing bullet made its way into the German front lines, tanks had become a heavy liability for all western commanders. Nowhere was this more proven than during the Battle of Cambrai in 1917. The Germans had been pushed back many miles by a heavy joint effort of infantry, artillery, air support and armored "landships." The Germans counter attacked at the right time and forced an immediate three-mile march back into English lines to conclude the bloody battle. Due to Germany's ability to label and address a weakness by devising a counter, they were able to capture a large number of British tanks during the effort. This capture allowed Germany to technologically advance faster than the British had when developing the tank itself and ultimately lead to the legendary German tank innovations of the following three decades.

It is simply a matter of labeling and addressing the weakness inherent within your individual self. By addressing the weakness and devising a counter to that weakness rather than trying to keep up with the struggles of that weakness will save you time and money. Potentially your counter can be so efficient that it can lead to another garnered strength to be used by your repertoire of already harnessed strengths, no longer hampering your abilities. Your weaknesses pour into your entrepreneurial endeavor and your conscious understanding of that weakness paired with effort made to counter in any way possible will ensure that you and your business are not the subject of a forgotten war.

Twelve

Alliances and Dependencies

A VERY IMPORTANT PERSON in my life once told me that "no man is an island". During a time in my life of growing independence and competence, it was this advice that headed my full attention. I would sit and dwell on the words, thinking back to experiences of past hurt and disappointment in my own relationships. Are we all living on a single island, fighting and clawing for the limited resources around us? No man or woman can possibly be an island based on how all people need to depend on one another for support. Family, friends, peers, acquaintances, coworkers, clients and bosses all depend upon one another for different needs, and only a fool would be the first to admit emotion wasn't a powerful factor in any of these interactions.

When we build relationships with fellow humans, we exhibit infinite degrees of caution, indulgence and over-exposure. At the end of the day, it is the individual who is most able to discern positive from negative relationships who will have the most abundant and most bountiful relationships.

This era of history remains one of my favorites and is rich with examples directly relating to the way the world still spins today. Chronologically, this time period was as close to World War I as we are today. It was the dawn of the early modern world when men and women of non-noble birth can rise to the ranks of imperial rulers in the Western World. The Monarch's had ruled for centuries under the protection of the very fabric which sowed their own gluttonous privilege; the hearts and minds of lower born men and women. Spain in the early 19th century was the personification of European monarch rule. Charles IV was the rightful ruler and king of the Spanish empire, which was an expansive empire and had been one of the prominent powers in colonialist Europe up until the late 18th century.

The closest ally of Spain's was no other than Napoleon Bonaparte, who since 1804 had been the self-crowned Emperor of France. Napoleon earned his crown through war, politics and ambition. It is without doubt that while Napoleon was fighting his wars against a coalition of nations, Spain as an ally to Napoleon, was interested in protecting what was left of their great empire. The British were a villainous nation to the Spanish who had been a rival colonialist power for a few hundred years at this point. The Spanish had suffered major defeats against the British in 1805 and had lost optimum access to one of their core competencies as an empire. They lost control over the new world colonies.

Spain during the early 19th century, while Napoleon was fighting and winning central Europe, dealt with a great degree of internal and external strife. Spain was under a constant threat of invasion and harassment by the British and the close British ally; the Portuguese. It was to no surprise that Napoleon and Charles IV had devised a plan to invade Portugal around 1806 after Napoleon had all but cemented his power in modern eastern Germany.

In order to assist Spain, Napoleon started the preparations for an invasion of Portugal. This meant organizing, training and sending troops down to Spain to await a future invasion. Spain was in a desperate position and the only perceived way out was to amass more territory and to remove the ongoing British threat from the Iberian Peninsula. It was with great luck that Spain had an ally in the North, France, to assist in abolishing the largest threat to the Spanish Monarchy, the British.

There are times in life when you have to be prepared to be betrayed. As an entrepreneur, you have to be ready for a relationship going south fast, even past the point of harm. You have to be sensing and knowing your areas of weakness at all times, even when it may seem like a major victory has just been won.

Due to the increasing number of foreign troops in the impoverished nation with no actual sign of gainful action towards an actual invasion, Spain started to turn in upon itself. The problems at large very quickly became a lot smaller to the men and women directly under the rule of the Spanish Monarchy. Charles IV eventually became vulnerable within his own citadel without the British ever having conducted an offensive inland action. The Spanish people became the biggest enemy to the Monarchy, and therefore overthrew Charles IV.

What happened next will have ramifications we can still feel today. Charles IV went directly to Napoleon, whose troops sat by and watched as Charles IV was dismantled as the ruling monarch. Napoleon forced Charles IV to abdicate his thrown to Napoleon and the French Empire. The once strong alliance very quickly turned into the complete destruction of the once great Spanish monarchy. Spain was thrust into a series of civil wars and British and French invasions. This was all while the once glorious Spanish new world was collapsing from threats within and without. The Peninsular Wars carried Spain through the next generation of young men and women, eventually being one of Napoleon's greatest failures as a ruler and as a general.

When we as entrepreneurs are faced with the need to engage in professional relationships, it is so important you do so with your 110 percent. Whether it be something minor or an issue terrifyingly important, the dependencies we must rely on can have altercations beyond what we can comprehend in the present. Humans are extremely complex beings with complex ambitions. How we place ourselves at risk is absolutely subject to the complex relationships involved with the process at hand. No one man or woman ever became a legend without depending on the people around them.

In today's age of highly technical communication, the alliances you build are few compared to the number of potential enemies that exist waiting for a time to take advantage of your weak maneuvers. Without a doubt, technology brings out relationships that we never would have had a chance to engage in without the presence of an application to speak our voice. That digital presence is a voice that carries the conjecture towards a man or woman's true personal intentions. It is face to face that we humans can ensure friends remain allies and allies remain dependable.

If your social media platform removes all effort necessary to have the perception of human relationships, and if you believe that you as a fellow human are a complex creature, then there is little doubt that the effort of your actions speak louder than the words you type on your phone.

Thirteen

Trust as a Weakness

"COMMERCE WITH ALL nations, alliance with none, should be our motto." -Thomas Jefferson

Very few times in history have alliances meant more to the receiver than to the pursuer. Typically, history books and media angles portray the alliance between two people or nations as mutually beneficial. This stance is often taken simply as a conclusive outcome of the partnership due to the negotiating table holding a mutual beneficial pact as the initial and ultimate goal of the pursuit. It is only through understanding the individual party's interests and in hindsight, when we have the advantage of understanding truly why two groups dealt the hands they did.

In the mid-18th century, there was a long-forgotten war that was waged between four major factions. The French and Native American tribes of North America versus the British Empire and its protectorate colonialist nation of America.

Imagine a war that changed the landscape of warfare forever, a war that took everything that was sophisticated about European conflict and shattered it entirely. The way wars had been fought by Europeans up until this point were controlled and mandated by the ruling officer classes. Rank and file meant rank and file.

This story wasn't brought forward to explain how warfare itself was revolutionized for European combatants fighting in North America. This story is about the men and women who sacrificed everything on a whim of trust between themselves and their extremely powerful European occupiers. The French and the

British had two entirely different methods of engaging the Native American tribal nations during the 17th and 18th centuries. While the British dominated their equation with malicious, aggressive and destructive actions, the French were cunning and conniving when building relationships with Native American tribal leaders.

The French were able to very quickly control a large land base in the new world due to their workings with the Native American tribes, rather than direct annihilation, like what the British and their colonialists employed. The French moved into North America with the intent to gain material riches through trading western goods for furs and information. Due to the French methods of working with the Native American, French Europeans were far less likely to make the travel to settle the new world compared to their British rivals. Therefore, by the time the Seven Year War began in the 1750s the French had a combined population of around 75,000, compared to around 1.5 million settlers the British Empire had at their disposal within the eastern colonies.

This inherent weakness was only known too well by the French colonial leaders. The French were masters of the modern gentlemanly styles of military engagement. In order for the French to win this war, a 'less civil' method of fighting had to become commonplace among French line troops. The key to this pursuit was the alliance with the Native American tribes who had been successfully implementing this guerilla style of warfare 'Le Petite Guerre'.

Since the French and the Native American tribal nations had already built a seemingly working relationship with one another, the pursuit of forming a cohesive alliance was very plausible. When looking at the equation from the Native American perspective, the argument for, or against, alliance seemed to solve itself. The French were a first world power that could provide all of the first world commodities in exchange for the Native American tribes to provide bodies for fighting. The English and their colonialists were an aggressive group the Native Americans saw inevitable conflict with. Also, the French made it appear that coexistence upon the land was the ultimate goal, compared to the English who viewed the Native American with unparalleled inferiority. The French were masters at appearing to hold more bargaining chips than they had when it came to Native American tribal politics.

From the Native American point of view, an alliance with the French meant an alliance of unprecedented strength against the English aggressor. Once the war officially broke out, the French and Native American alliance had experienced some major victories against the English colonies. The French had also proven their martial prowess by learning and mastering the guerilla style of warfare conducted by the Native American warrior nations. This allowed for the French to execute a much more effective engagement against an opponent with overwhelming numbers.

As the years went on, it had become ever more apparent the French commanders had to depend more and more on the Native American tribal nations to do the bulk of the fighting. The war was lost for the French once the English had cut off the French in North America from Europe by taking major holdings in Quebec and conclusively at Fort Niagara. During years of fighting alongside and taking many English forts, the Native American tribes had been subjected to heavily destructive diseases, such as smallpox, and rampant cultural division with the French. The years of fighting not only demonstrated the cultural differences between the French and the Native Americans in every way, but this hard reality came to fruition at the expense of the Native Americans in their homeland.

Once the French had abandoned North America, the once great Native American tribal nations of the Ohio River Valley, Mississippi River Valley and the Western Appalachian mountain regions had been bled out and left to die. The French used the Native American nations to fight a war of attrition they had little hope of winning in the first place. While the tactics employed by the French and the Native American alliance had its fair share of victories, many battles do not win a war of attrition against an overwhelming and superior force. While the French were able to retreat to their European mother nation, their Native American allies were left in a state if ill-reputed distress.

One of the major reasons this story has been forgotten is because the war itself has always appeared more honorable than the atrocities and genocides of Caucasian settlers over the vast expanse of time since the first pioneers had sailed to the new world. The mindset of the Native American leadership before the onset of the war saw little to lose joining forces with a seemingly powerful nation like New France. From the Native American point of view, there was choosing between one Caucasian with a gun or another Caucasian with a gun and a smile. The French had pursued a relationship far more amiably than the British, but it was this exact method of exploitation that allowed the French to subject the Native American nations to fight a war with little chance of success. To the French it was a numbers game, to the English it was an opportunity and to the Native American it was life or death.

Let's bridge this 250-year-old story with our modern day entrepreneurial culture and lifestyles. This specific story rings home to my heart and to many individuals walking down the road of entrepreneurial engagement. Developing products, ideas and initiatives takes an unarguable amount of risk and sacrifice to acquire. The hunger for success is equivalent to the hunger for survival, and all adamant entrepreneurs put it all on the line in order to see their pursuits properly executed. It is this necessity for survival and success that drives all entrepreneurs across the planet.

There are fewer items in an entrepreneur's arsenal of weapons that allow themselves the perceived power to have control over the destiny of their entrepreneurial endeavor when a venture capitalist or an angel investor walks in the door. It is hard for an individual or small team with no resources to pass up and argue against an investor talking big dollars in accord to this seemingly strong alliance. This initial sense of superiority gives venture capitalists and angel investors ultimate power over the average entrepreneur.

Entering a partnership with any investor requires more than just pitch decks and equity guarantees. Every entrepreneur should consider a few crucial factors before ever locking arms with an external investor. Evaluating the personal relationship between the entrepreneur and the investor, the investor's applicable industry knowledge and the investor's capability and willingness to provide long term support through failure and success are essential for an entrepreneur and investor to succeed together. The wise entrepreneur will tell you that if you have a product worth investing into by an external party, then you already have a product worth your time of investment.

Most entrepreneurs seeking investment do so due to lack of resources or lack of ability to move forward without outside help. This is a common problem that all entrepreneurs must face the reality of, but it is also one of the easiest cliffs to fall from. Driving a product from point A to point B with the inability to drive to point C does not make your product worth where it could be at point C. This is the logic most investors will approach you with in order to drive more equity and more control out of you. The time you have invested into your product while standing on your own two feet is only equivalent to the check written by someone sitting at a desk if the foresight is present to predict and to prepare against the relationship's eventual downfalls. If this foresight is not present, you should prepare to lose what you have worked so hard to achieve, or you should never enter into such an uneasy alliance.

Fourteen

Why Capitalism?

IT IS WITHOUT A DOUBT one of the most cliché arguments to make in today's age. Over the past century, there has been a very obvious war being waged between communist and capitalist rule within emerging economies of the world. I personally have always found either side of this argument to be an interesting platform to stand on because time and time again communism has befallen all of the same downfalls which plague that of capitalism. The issues don't necessarily derive from either system directly but rather from the weak areas which plague all systems and people. Capitalism has always just survived the onslaught when communism usually leads to mass graves.

There is one story that stands out above all the others when it comes to demonstrating the weaknesses inherent within all systems, while also showing how communism breaks while capitalism bends.

Mao Zedong will always be considered one of the most influential and revolutionary individuals to have ever lived in modern era history. His rise to power is parallel with the evolution of China during the early 20th century, and it can be easily argued that his leadership style became so authoritarian that repercussions will reverberate throughout the course of world history for centuries to come.

The revolutionary political party gained control of the long-time imperialist nation of China right after World War II, which transformed China into an isolationist communist nation. After Mao gained power as the overall leader of the single political party which ruled China, he very quickly transformed his position into an autocratic one. With very little hesitation, Mao's most influential decision was the restructuring of China from a primarily agricultural state to an industrial powerhouse.

One of the first actions undertaken by Mao's autocratically communist party was the acquisition and monopolization of every agricultural vertical across the entire country. The government was in control of everything from production, harvest, collection, processing and redistribution. It was the intent of the government to take control of the entire vertical process so agriculture could be better managed, food could be properly produced and forceful rationing would eliminate over-indulgence. Farming communities were slowly consolidated from single family units into collectives of a number of family units. These collectives eventually grew in size and complexity as the years went on.

Following this massive restructuring of the agricultural infrastructure of the country, the nation began its quest to become the largest industrial powerhouse in the world. Mao's regime decided to move a large portion of the agricultural workforce into more urban and industrialized areas. This move was very important to the achievement of the industrialization goal due to optimistic quotas set forth by top bureaucrats. The major population shift left the shrinking agricultural base under-staffed and the growing non-agricultural base just as hungry.

While the redirection of the working class and the monopolization of the entire agricultural infrastructure had made logical sense at the time, the quick movement of these changes caused unparalleled damages across the country to the agricultural output of the nation. This was multiplied by the government taking charge of all aspects of agricultural managerial decisions on behalf of the farming communities. Bureaucratic process became the new way to manage all agricultural issues and decisions. Instead of the pro-active management the agricultural industry needs to avoid the inevitable drought seasons, the bureaucratic monopolization of the entire industry caused a hyper-slow reactive management of the nation's food resources. Finally, the bureaucratic influencers having been put in charge were more educated in the intricacies of politics rather than the humble complexities of farming. The incompetence of the bureaucratic monopoly running the entire agricultural vertical spelled vast and grave consequences for the nation as a whole.

It is estimated that during Mao Zedong's rule, tens of millions of people died due to bureaucratic mismanagement. This period of time has gone down in the record books as one of the most prominent catastrophes in world history. Some scholars say this atrocity was worse than Hitler's invasion of Poland and the Japanese invasion of Manchuria during World War II. Mao's communism not only caused the starvation of an entire fraction of his own population, but also played a crucial hand in destroying much of the history and culture of ancient China during the process. China lost much of its ancestral history under Mao Zedong. All of this was due to the autocratic and communist regime placed in charge over the nation, which had given control of macro-decision making to idealistic overlords and micro-decision making to incompetent bureaucrats.

It is easy to find a positive example for comparison to a story with such a horrific conclusion. It is actually probably one of the easiest things to do when discussing Mao Zedong's Great Leap Forward. What is more difficult is to find an example of 21st century American capitalist politics that has a comparable objective to the monopolistic endeavors of Mao's regime. There are dozens of examples where the U.S. government has attempted to directly engage in the business and organizational practices of some of our largest industry players. The auto industry and banking industry bailouts of the late 2000s, the re-focus towards militarization of American industry during World War II and of course, the most recent Affordable Care Act under Barack Obama. All of these examples in American history demonstrate a time when the U.S. federal government needed to take autocratic steps at controlling an industry to a desired end. These examples can be considered very similar to the actions taken by Mao towards the Chinese agricultural and industrial sectors.

There is a simple major difference when it comes to the Mao initiative compared to all of the American examples of industry controlled by bureaucratic regime. The simple difference is the continued privatization of the ownership equity within each industry. In the U.S. capitalist system, when a governing body moves in to take autocratic steps at forcing change upon an industry, the government takes measures to move around the invariable private ownership interest present within that sector. For example, the Affordable Care Act forces members to purchase from private insurance participants. This single effort of ensuring capitalist ideology stays present within each sector of the U.S. economy is one of the best reasons for why when other nations break due to bureaucratic incompetence, the United States will bend when facing this same incompetence. The variable in the communist capitalist equation is not that one nation's bureaucracy is more or less incompetent than the other. The variable in the communist capitalist equation is that private sector ownership interest being held as a priority in the capitalist component trumps inept autocratic rule.

Fifteen

A Follower Makes a Leader

THE DESERT FOX. Those three simple words deserve their own sentence. The why, when and how of these three words describes some of this era's furthest achievements and most immoral degradations. Erwin Rommel started off his career like the most of us. He was an average student but a hard worker with high aspirations. He was born into a family of modest living, which gave him the grace of diligence and discipline.

In World War I, Rommel had time and time again proven his pure warrior heart and spirit through gleaming displays of courage and aggression. Very quickly, he rose through the ranks from a junior to a mid-level officer under the German monarchy. His prowess on the battlefield was not unlike many other legendary military figures of our long human history. The opportunity to prove his superior execution during pitched battle and success of that execution was at the mercy of the time in history for which his person stood. An argument can be made that the opportunity for war will create heroes while an opposite argument can also be made that only the present hero has the fate to solely define a war.

Erwin Rommel stayed in the military after the first world war, which was to his benefit and to the foreboding bereavement to an entire generation of people in the western world. Erwin Rommel spent these peacetime years honing the very sword that would cut through Europe like iron would water. It is without a doubt the literature written by Rommel during these years would give him the notoriety that would eventually lead him into a room with Adolf Hitler.

Hitler very quickly saw the greatness within Rommel, and once the Third Reich started to throw rocks in the pond, it was Rommel who made the greatest splash during the blitzkrieg of France. What once was a half-decade long stalemate along the Maginot Line, Field Marshal Rommel with the 7th Panzer Division had in a single offensive laid waste to the grinding warfare of World War I. This accomplishment created such a stir in the German public that Rommel was immediately lifted to legendary status. Hitler was heavily rewarded in the public eye for lifting Rommel up through the ranks and continued to exploit Field Marshal Rommel on the battlefield at any possible chance.

In early 1941 Rommel was given command of the North African campaign against the English occupiers. Rommel very quickly disposed of any resistance in the western region, all while he was able to gain significant ground against the English defending Egypt. It is obvious that Hitler gave Rommel possibly the most important single objective in the war; the capturing of The Middle East. If the Germans were able to occupy lands through Egypt and up through Persia, this would have provided a backdoor to the Russian heartland. Furthermore, the argument does not have to be made for the importance of oil when it comes to fueling the juggernaut panzer and panzer grenadier companies of the Third Reich. This swift move was imperative to Hitler's plans to occupy and hold all of Europe. Rommel was the key that unlocked a door for which tyrants had been competing over for many millennia.

The English had become increasingly desperate when facing Erwin Rommel. His ability to predict, exploit and counter-attack were almost unworldly. As the German war machine was advancing on key Egyptian cities, particularly Alexandria, it was the unseen aggressor who had taken Rommel out of power at the detest of Hitler. Rommel had become extremely physically ill and was shipped to Austria for recovery. Rommel stayed a close advisor to Hitler during these times. Also, this trip home had become the perfect opportunity for Hitler's opponents to seize one of Germany's greatest assets, Erwin Rommel and his public approval.

After Rommel had recovered, the legacy that was the German victory over North Africa was already a forgotten dream. The

English under new leadership and Rommel's absence, were able to quickly turn the tide of the war. At this same time, Rommel began to question Hitler's strategy and goals in open dialogue directly with Hitler. Unlike many in Nazi run Germany, Rommel commanded the respect of Hitler and had become one of the very few open denouncers of Hitler's Germany. It was obvious that a subsect of powerful German leaders came together to move forward with the downfall of Hitler. While many men cowered under subjugation, Rommel voiced his countermands to Hitler's strategies. It was at this moment Hitler had truly signed Germany's death note. If Hitler would have listened to Rommel and avoided the catastrophic invasion of foreign powers, Germany as a nation would have been saved. Instead of listening to quality followers, Hitler continued to embrace his ties with Nazi figureheads.

It must be said that Hitler was in a deeply ingrained position of sin and horror by the time 1944 rolled around. His action during the Third Reich goes down in history at the top of the list for indescribable genocidal, deprave and unfathomable actions against our fellow man and woman. The world as we know it changed under Hitler and men like Erwin Rommel were blessed with many gifts misdirected by a group's aggressive actions. The men who attempted to kill Hitler did so under subterfuge. They attempted to assassinate Hitler to ill-luck. Rommel approached Hitler directly with distaste. With Hitler instilling his 'fight to the death' law among the troops under Rommel's control, it was apparent that Hitler was going to take Germany down with him in a sea of flames.

While we can write entire libraries on why Hitler was an evil man, it is hard to imagine just how close Hitler had come to true world supremacy. In the end, Hitler could have at the very least avoided utter destruction if he had listened to his most honest associates. Rommel was forced to commit suicide under the eyes of the gestapo. Hitler ensured that any and all conspirators were either killed or allowed to commit honorable suicide. The track had been laid and the train had come through for Nazi Germany. The invasion lasted less than a year, and while Rommel was sitting in a grave with full military honors, Hitler's bull-headed approach at demagoguery ensured the destruction of old-world Germany.

This story leaves us in a place of discomfort with the title. Do we want a leader to win at the end? Usually in our business case studies, the leader is often a valiant man or woman. In this case, we discuss the pure existence of evil in history as the leader within our relationship spectrum. Rommel was the follower and a most accomplished follower at that, but nevertheless, a follower. Rommel knew the answer, and he had the courage to approach Hitler with the solution. This is the sign of a most honest and worthwhile follower. A follower who puts his career on the line for your own. We can hold a debate in under five seconds if the conversation is surrounding the moral choices of Hitler's regime, but from a pure follower/leadership analyses, Rommel was the answer for Hitler. Yet, Hitler chose the wrong group of followers to heed advice from.

This ability to discern quality followers from inadequate followers is probably one of the toughest skills to master in the leadership handbook. It is without question that it is imperative to the success of a leader. Having honest, focused, uncomfortable and action oriented feedback from followers can make or break a leader's agenda. Hitler was evil, there is no doubt. It is also without question that his empire could have lasted much longer if he had the ability to remove ignorance from his heart and poor followers from his board room.

Followership and leadership doesn't necessarily need to end in morally positive action. A leader is simply someone with followers and a follower is simply someone with a leader. The thoughts and goals of both are influenced equally by the other. Rommel's story tells us the story of a follower with power, even if the leader's demise is to the benefit of everyone else. The power in a follower under both circumstances is inarguably decisive.

Sixteen

A Life of Absolutes

THERE IS LITTLE DOUBT that our 21st century social structure has built an expectation that the most successful people in the world must make sacrifices to obtain such ambitions. Whether it be portrayed as a corporate powerhouse CEO working late hours at the office with no time for extroverted ventures, the hustling entrepreneur who has chosen to forgo romance for the sake of client engagement or the proud father and mother who have turned down the corner office promotions to ensure quality time is focused towards their own budding family. It is easy to write a movie script, post on social media or conclude a conversation with such absolutes. Society has made it quite clear that you must either choose success in business or success at home, both impede the other and neither will ever exist in perfect harmony.

In France from 1812 to 1813, the state of affairs was among perfection. In fact, one could make the argument to be a French man or woman in this era was both a sense of limitless pride overshadowed by impending vulnerability. The invasion of Russia in 1812 can easily be considered one of the few historic points of human awareness for the people of Europe. What Napoleon and the French were able to do was almost god-like in the eyes of the pre-modern world. Monarchy and republicanism were at the very center of the common dialogue of the time. Dinner tables with mothers, fathers, sons and daughters, held daily conversations based on these political views. The king or the republic? The empire or her people?

After the loss in Russia, the French people were exhausted from war, yet hell bent upon seeing its conclusion in their own favor. The machine that was the French empire under Napoleon lived solely to ensure the state's existence. The pride people can have for such accomplishments is nationalistic for its loyalty to the components of self-preservation.

It is easy to write entire collections of scrolls on such emotions of doom and disparity. While pride held the farm together, mortality was the ultimate exposure Napoleon forced his subjects and his enemies' subjects to embrace. Is war as hard on the leader of such actions compared to the legions of men and women who give their lives up for such undesirable consequences? The answer in turn lies in the mindset of the people in the times and their external motivating factors, such as nationalism.

Directly after the loss in Russia, Napoleon was able to amass an army large enough to conquer Europe over another time. With over 300,000 men guarding his still large empire, the War of the Sixth Coalition was still very much a long road to walk. The forces bearing down upon the French empire were as challenged as ever, yet the global knowledge of Napoleon's own mortality was won in the snows of Russia in 1812.

One can easily imagine the burden that was on a single man like Napoleon at this time. Any mistakes done in the past were inevitably going to conclude ill against both the name and soul of Napoleon Bonaparte. This is why Napoleon Bonaparte II was such an important component of Europe's self-preservation and self-actualization. The only son of Napoleon easily could be considered one of the great future dynastic lineages of the European Monarchy. This only maintained in post revolutionary France a comfortable position of embracing the dynastic traditions, easily apparent in French society, while also the post-revolutionary angle that all men and women are born with the ability to conquer through proven actions, which is what Napoleon I more than demonstrated.

Only the ignorant could imagine a world in which Napoleon I did not already see his lineage presented to the people of France in this way. It was the entire Bonaparte mindset to conclude power is earned through proven methodology. Napoleon's son was equally as important to his legacy as was his physical conquest over Europe when taken into perspective as of 1813. Napoleon's love and admiration of his son is reminiscent of all parents and their children. Napoleon's legendary actions play no difference to the equation of the family unit. Time invested into children reward parents on both a supernatural and natural level. Napoleon I was not ignorant to this logic.

Napoleon's specific interaction with his child is recorded from historical accounts of the two individuals' relationship. Napoleon would often jump on the floor to see his son, frolic in courtyards whilst his son played and often would playfully tease his son like any father would. The relationship existed because the time existed. Napoleon made the time to interact with his son. Napoleon would often hold his son during military meetings for example. The absolute separation of work and family was not present within Napoleon's life. The energy was directed towards influencing his child when an opportunity would arise.

This was not just an absolute from the perspective of invested time towards raising a child. The demand for a heavy investment into Napoleon's Empire was always present. The family unit in fact was driven around Napoleon's career to a point in which Napoleon was at the obvious center of attention. The point none the less stands that time was made to play a role within the life of a child, ahead of just pure selfish interest, even if the world Napoleon built was catered to him. The absolute did not exist in either the personal or professional perspective. Napoleon did not believe in absolute conclusions other than the ones he personally created. Therefore, any man or woman with enough inhibition to strive to walk through life with equally apparent absence of absolute conclusions, has the power to do the same.

There are no absolutes that cater to happiness. Life is about the little things that you make time to enjoy. If absolutes are your track to happiness then you will miss many of the positive experiences life may have to offer you, much like Napoleon and his ability to enjoy his own son's dynastic opportunity. While it is impossible to achieve any desired level of success, personal or professional, without sacrifice, focusing on life's conclusions as a series of absolutes is not the formula for perfect balance and harmony. Balance and harmony in one's life maximizes the optimum potential for all personal and professional qualities one may garner.

Seventeen

Character of a True Friend

WHAT DEFINES A TRUE FRIEND? There are numerous ways one can define the qualities that go into a valuable and worthwhile relationship with another individual. Ultimately, it is up to both parties to approach the other with a balance of openness, loyalty and energy in order to derive a fruitful relationship out of nothing. There is a single common aspect that all relationships with promise possess that can lead someone into entering either a long-lasting worthwhile friendship or an inevitably doomed partnership. This commonality, which always appears at the beginning of any professional and personal relationships, is a shared common goal.

In Eastern Europe during the late 11th century, a powerful foe existed seeking the occupation and destruction that was the way of life in the Christian Roman Empire. The Muslim Turkish people had been for centuries a plague on Christendom, so much so that the very fabric of Roman legacy was beginning to crumble where it once stood tall. The Byzantine Empire, up to this time, was a fraction of its once glorious position after having suffered incessant defeats at the hands of the Muslim armies of Anatolia, Egypt and the Eastern Mediterranean. Under Emperor Alexius, the Byzantine Empire possessed no army of significance, no money and faced an inevitable invasion of the Muslim factions across the Sea of Marmara.

Against the longstanding prideful tradition of self-sustainability that the Byzantine Emperors had up to this point, Emperor Alexius sent out a cry for help to the Western Roman Empire under the leadership of Pope Urban II. The Pope spent no time in deliberation over the tenants of this request. The conversations with other leaders of the Western Roman Empire were organized to ensure a uniform conversation in order to address the threats coming from the Muslim states. It was eventually decided that the Western Roman Empire under the decree of Pope Urban II would assist Emperor Alexius and his Byzantine Empire in combating this threat. The first ever crusade was initiated in order to take back Jerusalem from the Muslim occupiers and the conversion over to the ways of Jesus Christ any and all willing.

As word spread across Europe like wildfire, princes, dukes, nobles, knights and even the peasant class rallied to the banner of the Roman Catholic Church to embark on such a holy and benign quest. As the ruling class was slow to muster the organized armies of Western Europe, the lower peasant class lead by lowborn knights and nobles had a head start in making the long journey east. One particular leader of this "crusade of the poor people" was Peter the Hermit, an aged soldier and brilliant leader, able to muster upwards of 40,000 men, women and children. There were few knights and even fewer professional soldiers within this lot of the lowest of classes from this era of history. As this horde marched its way across Western Europe, ahead of the professional armies, spirits were high and actions were justified.

It wasn't until the large band of people began marching across Hungary that things started to slip south. This large of a group required an immense supply of resources by locals as they traveled through the Eastern European region. Looting, pillaging, devastation and retribution were inevitable as scuffles with the local Hungarian population continued. By the time Peter the Hermit and his horde of loyal followers reached Constantinople, the total number of peasant crusaders numbered around 30,000. As the Emperor Alexius first witnessed the arrival of this horde, his prayers for a professional army remained unanswered. The risk of instability within Constantinople for allowing such an unorganized and chaotic horde of people to stay too long was quickly addressed. The Emperor hastily agreed to and organized the methods in which the men, women and children under Peter the Hermit would be transported across the Sea of Marmara and into the heart of the Muslim occupied peninsula.

Almost immediately after the unarmed band of peasant crusaders established a presence on the peninsula, harassment by Turkish bows and swords began. Any unorganized raids by the crusaders into Muslim lands were vastly futile compared to the lightning fast professional responses by Turkish cavalry. Eventually, when hopes had become low, Peter the Hermit returned to Constantinople in order to plead with the Emperor for assistance in saving the people under his care. The divine shield of the Christian God that was supposed to protect the host of the people's crusade successfully to Jerusalem instead lead every participant onto the end of a sword or to be sold into slavery by the Turks.

This grand quest had everything affixed to its perspective to be considered an undertaking by an alliance of individuals seeking a common goal. There was a real and dire threat presented to the people of the Roman Empire, and a response was very much justifiable on the grounds of self-preservation. The Emperor Alexius with the most to lose from the onset of this story, pleaded for assistance. His calls for a professional army were answered by the passionate yet unsuccessful horde of lower class peasants led by Peter the Hermit and eventually by many of the princes of the west who succeeded in their quest of conquering Jerusalem. Lastly, it was under the banner of Pope Urban II that these men, women and children were able to justify joining a crusade to the holy land. The man who represents Saint Peter at the head of the Catholic Church has the power to amass untold devotion from his followers.

If we understand that all three of the individuals within this story shared a common goal, we can begin to understand how each of their characters played a hand in dealing the cards that would signify the eventual annihilation of the people's crusade. Before we do this analysis, it is important to state this component of the formula. If friendship is defined by the character of both parties within the relationship, therefore the most important component to labeling another person's strength of character is that individual's actions in the face of a specific ruleset.

Let us start with Pope Urban II who had signaled the banners, rallied the masses, abated internal conflict and ultimately signaled the start of the crusading era. This individual obviously possessed a common goal in line with the men, women and children who marched in the people's crusade, and his actions were very much directly in line with the expectations of these same people. If his actions and intentions were sound, then the only alarming component of his position, in turn eliminating his quality of character, was the convenience his actions held within the weight of his decision. Sitting on a comfy cushion in Rome is a lot easier of place to rest when sending tens of thousands of people to their graves. It was this lack of inconvenience that defines the level of Pope Urban II's character and ultimately this character fault is what betrays the crusading people.

Next there stands a man of the utmost opulence in the middle ages, the Emperor Alexius of Byzantium. This man did not particularly have the luxury to make a decision as conveniently as Pope Urban II did on his throne in Rome. The Emperor was directly and consistently under threat of annihilation. Therefore, one can easily make the assumption of a common goal with the crusading host being present. It wasn't until the Emperor's calls for help had been answered, and the horde of peasant crusaders were quickly approaching the lands of the Byzantine Empire until Alexius's true character was revealed. At this point, the Emperor was given an opportunity to put action where his intentions were presented. The Emperor immediately took the position of addressing the short-term inconvenience of hosting such a chaotic horde within his lands and wasted no time in ferrying the members of the people's crusade into hostile lands.

Finally, there is the charismatic Peter the Hermit, who without a doubt played a crucial and clever hand in guiding the fate of his followers while sharing a common goal with the Pope's message. Few characters in history make me wonder why a movie hasn't been made yet about his life story compared to Peter the Hermit. His role in amassing a host of disorganized peasants and low-born knights was enough to stand the test of time. It can be said that in a time when only the wealthiest of nobles could ever imagine gathering such power behind their sword arm, Peter did just that.

His actions, his efforts and his results all spoke leagues about the character he was to the peasants undertaking this crusade. If he was 98% of the way towards perfectly demonstrating his character, as a friend and ally of the people, then why does the remaining 2% carry more water? It is simply because the self-gain that Peter the Hermit experienced during this time displayed a heavy light upon the true character of the man. His rags to riches story, the increasing presence at the Emperor's court and his pursuit of wartime monetary gains spelled out the true character overshadowed by the results of his actions towards the common goal.

In conclusion, character is the optimum definition of another individual's friendship, alliance and predicted ambition. In order to obtain confidence in a friend, one must obtain a demonstration of character. Character is derived by proving intent towards a common goal with action and analyzing said action against the backdrop of their current position. Any lack of inconvenience followed by swift action towards a shared goal, whether results are positive or negative, does not prove out an individual's character. Effective actions toward a common goal that claim origin upon short-term inconvenience of the acting party to otherwise not act do not prove an individual's character. Any action that either is convenient or provides individualized gain to the acting party, separate from the party's gain, does not prove out a person's character. True character finds origin by labeling a pursuit towards a common goal, followed by an action demonstrating inconvenience to the acting party, without the semblance of personal gain disassociated with the original common goal.

Eighteen

How to Judge a Subordinate

THERE IS ALWAYS THE constant presence of judgement in any relationship. Whether this judgement formulates itself as simply as the recognition of an un-ironed shirt or as hypocritical as blatant racism driven by ignorance and bigotry. Judgement is commonplace for human thought processes; the concept has governed the realm of relationship building since humans could compare rock throwing efficiency. For the purpose of this chapter, we are only going to focus on the level of judgement that one needs to embrace in order to be an effective leader within the professional setting when interacting with subordinates.

There is a lot to be said about having the courage to act during a window of opportunity, while not acting would risk a large reward. This window of opportunity was exactly what built The United States of America from the ashes of British colonialism during the 18th century. Great men and women fought hard to obtain even the slightest opportunity to create a country that would eventually become the greatest embodiment of everything just within our world. The fight to achieve this opportunity was grueling, risky beyond imagination and counter-intuitive to everything the world of that age had understood to be feasible. While it can be said that France led the way in terms of republicanism, it was The United States that truly signaled the death of the monarchs.

Entire libraries have been written around the adversities overcome by the founders of the USA. The political, social, economic and other prevailing issues of the time were all material components in how this country successfully obtained its independence. Nowhere was there more sacrifice and leadership demonstrated than on the battlefield during the American Revolution. The men that gave their lives for the chance at freedom were the true risk takers. In fact, most of these men had no ability to influence the results of their labor in the formation of the U.S. as a government. Nevertheless, many fought and died for the faith in what this country could become behind strong leadership.

The American continental army was first established using volunteers in a slightly more organized fashion than was common for the average regional militias and other armed citizenry. When General George Washington took control of the military situation, the continental army was barely even an army at all. Funding was poor, which lead to ill-equipped, malnourished and demoralized troops. At times during the war, the British propaganda machine coupled with numerous losses by the Americans left much of the civilian population at home either questioning or directly absolving support for the war. When taking into consideration the standard military effectiveness of line troops at the time, the American units were below substandard at best. There was so little organization within the army camps, they often would be built without any management, and men would relieve themselves wherever they so well pleased. From a military discipline perspective, this was the bottom of the barrel.

The British Army, under the command of General Henry Clinton, was the epitome of global martial prowess. Having just gained unparalleled success after the Seven Years War, The British Empire was at its peak of colonial power. Naval dominance in the Atlantic was one of the premier strengths the British possessed going into the American War for Independence. Over 40,000 armed professional troops were garrisoned across the continental states. These troops were experienced, hardened, loyal to the death, had full support from the homeland, supplies were adequate, moral was high, discipline was ensured, and the uniforms were pristine. From an outside observer, the British troops looked exactly how a well-oiled military machine should. Another large benefit of the British troops was the fact that many of the American subjects were still a proponent of, or at least on the fence, in support of the British monarchy. If the American continental army in this period could be demonstrated by a single representative, that individual would be soft-spoken, timid and boorish. The British Army would be an individual demonstrating proud, confident and vociferous qualities.

If we were to sit back and judge the effectiveness each of the armies would have been predicted to exhibit from the onset of the war, we would have easily been a proponent for the British and would have dismissed the rabble under the command of General George Washington. Not only did the British Army on paper have an actual physical and moral advantage compared to the Americans, they also had a resume of success and discipline that would back that theory up as well. There is in fact very little to base an argument on that would have given the Americans an advantage to win the war if we were simply playing an outside judge at the onset of the war.

As the war progressed, it had become clear just how badly the cards had been stacked against the continental army. Many of the aforementioned disadvantages faced by the common American troop had actually become visible, there was little hiding the uphill war that was being waged by the men who had originally signed the U.S. Constitution.

Based upon our already mentioned obvious judgements of the situation the common observer would have made and if we didn't benefit from an application of hindsight, we would have been terribly wrong. One of the major surprises to any outside observer, and very much so a surprise to King George at the time, was the eventual surrender of British occupation in 1781. The reasoning for such an astounding and unanticipated victory for the American colonies can give us an ideal look into what we will be able to derive as an application of reasonable judgement when attempting to inject such a theory of prediction to a more modern and professional setting.

The American troops believed in the potential for an optimal conclusion because leaders like George Washington engaged the men on a personal and emotional level, through inspiring leadership. Eventually, this engagement made the troops believe they could actually do it. This, combined with the work ethic and determination of the common trooper, propelled by their heart being in the leadership, the game plan and the general cause for the war, gave the American continental soldier the will and strength to achieve the objective. Leadership was the most crucial component from the viewpoint of the common soldier. Leadership that demonstrated competence, winning battles, and loyalty, exemplified in the public image by George Washington crossing the river Delaware with his men, ensured that the troops willing to be lead, were done so effectively.

The British soldier on the other hand, with the most optimum starting position in this scenario, was unable to find consistent affirmation within the leadership available to them. The attrition of war with the Americans and an eventual inability for the British Navy to demonstrate the superiority of British influence abroad lead to surrender. Last but not least, the demoralization due to lackluster leadership through the inability by the general staff to address a need for change in tactical direction. The British generals continued to fight a war that was based within the rules of Western European conflict, instead of the guerilla maneuvers the American generals learned to adopt.

To get to the conclusion of how to judge a subordinate effectively, while it is important to take into consideration the direct potential for a subordinate to complete a task, there is a deeper and more worthwhile quality in individuals that can propel even the most lackluster of participants to the forefront. This quality lies within the subordinate's willingness to be lead, their energy, work ethic and heart in the objective. Even the most under-classed participant will have an opportunity for success if they meet these four criteria. Now, if you would combine someone with the repertoire of a prodigy into the body of an individual with these four qualities, then you may have a legendary character on your hands. If you are able to obtain a predetermination of these qualities using reasonable judgement within a subordinate, you will have a worthwhile and fruitful relationship pursuing whatever task may lie ahead. Pair this with competent and engaging leadership, there are few qualified subordinates that will not obtain the opportunity to be a successful component to any professional team.

Nineteen

When Loyalty Lies

THERE IS A LOT TO be said about the loyalty of an employee under your jurisdiction. A loyal individual is someone who you will be able to command the respect of in order to achieve a desired result. To command an individual's respect is to fight side by side and against all odds without hesitation, most notably because this follower is someone who wants to be led by that person. There is another type of respect harnessing that can be masked as a form of commanding of respect but always follows through to a less worthwhile process and an eventual weaker conclusion.

In the 5th century B.C., there existed a culture unlike anything we have in the modern world, a culture of pure martial dominance. Martial prowess was ingrained within every aspect of life, from social, political, and even economic. The family unit was designed to optimize the capability of the warrior class, and children were either bred to be warriors or were bred to breed more warriors. There was no unnecessary time spent on tasks not focused upon strengthening the Spartan soldier's martial stature.

The Spartan lifestyle was minimalist to an extreme. Everything and anything was subjugated in order to provide for the elite warrior class, this included land, resources and conquered people. Helots were the slaves of ancient Sparta, most of them conquered and subjugated by the elite warrior class. During the original development of Sparta, the rich and fertile region of Messenia was dominated by the Spartans. This region was well suited for agriculture and had a thriving population of free people which took care of the lands for the Spartans in exchange for protection. At one point, the Spartan nobility decided the freedom allotted these people had run its course, the Messenian men were therefore butchered and the rest were enslaved as helots. This was the Spartan way of the life, subjugation and dominance.

While the Spartan men were solely focused on martial glory or politics, the Spartan women focused on home economy and childbearing, the helots were in charge of everything else. Fielding crops, managing infrastructure, professional trades and other day to day labor beneath Spartan men and women. In fact, Spartan men were not allowed by law to engage in economic trades, instead leaving these tasks for the helot underlings. The helot population, as you could imagine, was such a crucial component to the well-being of Sparta that the entire military support infrastructure was dependent upon the labors of the helot slave populace. This way of life was self-sustaining, refined and staunchly efficient to the goals of the Spartan free men and women.

Not all things are perfect and neither was this way of life for the Spartans. Due to the helot population being involved in such a micro and macro level of utilization in the Spartan society, the risk of the helots revolting was constant and often. The risk was so great that at one point the ablest bodied fighting men of the helot population were told to gather together for the opportunity to earn their freedom by fighting alongside the Spartan legions in battle. When the fighting men gathered to pledge loyalty to the king, the Spartan soldier class put every helot man to death. This was done simply to quell any threat of rebellion in the coming seasons. Additionally, on an annual basis, the Spartan Council of Elders would declare war upon the helot population, so murdering slaves would not be considered illegal. This gave the Spartan people the ability to constantly keep the helot slave population in check.

All of this dependence upon the helot people came with the downside of having to spend large investments of time by the Spartan men and women in keeping the helot people in line with their slave status. This constant need to be present around the helots and stomp out revolts before coming to fruition would become the Achilles heel of the Spartan people. Having the martial capability to invade and conquer any and all lands that existed across the Mediterranean at that time, meant very little when the Spartan soldiers were unable to leave their home for any reasonable extended period of time. What had become the Spartans greatest strength; for this infrastructure allowed the Spartan people to become the supreme warrior class in the world, was also their greatest weakness, which prevented the Spartan dominance of far reaching lands.

In the modern world, it is hard to imagine an organization or a company that would treat their units of employees with as much barbaric and malicious contempt. The actions allowed in this ancient time period have been completely abolished by the enforced universal ethical laws of humanity. Some people could make an argument that these humane laws just came about during this last century. This doesn't mean the inability to contextually understand a similarity to modern corporations with their seas of employees, instead of enslaved helots. Today, corporations support billions of human beings across the planet and do so with much of same minimalist objectives as the Spartans in antiquity. Employees day in and day out support the infrastructure of an organization to support an elitist hierarchy of management, all souls focused towards the overall objective of shareholder value.

There is the same potential today though to wield either a standard axe by the handle or to accept the fate of the double-edged sword. The Spartans wielded this sword with barbaric pride and glory. Corporations that treat their employees more like assets on a balance sheet than a human with a soul suffer the exact same fate as the stubborn Spartan overseers. Organizations with poorly motivated, rudely treated employees living consistently impoverished lifestyle conditions do not command the respect of their workforce. One poor move by management and the employee population could revolt, spelling doom for an organization's profitability, sustainability and ultimately shareholder value.

Modern employee revolts in the 21st century really only have one difference in comparison to the helots, that being the non-violent retribution for such actions against the well-being of the company or management of said company. Today employees leave organizations and wind up causing issues of high turnover within the growing workforce. Also, poor quality of work by said workforce due to lack of motivation is apparent. In certain industries, employees will strike and often refuse work. Poor company culture will eventually lead to poor team chemistry and communication. Companies that do not respect work/life balances for employees end up having weaker employees in the long run. There are a number of other examples of poor relationship status between company and employee that will cause a direct retribution to the bottom line.

Much like the Spartans and their helots, employees are both the greatest asset and the biggest risk to the management at a company. With strong employees comes very strong performance to the shareholders, to the benefit of management. Yet negative and aggressive pressure upon the workforce, with responses of harsh judgement, leaves a company weak and foolish. The greatest companies in the world do so with a workforce that believes in the organization on an almost spiritual level, not in obligation or with threats spread with the fist. We have grown a lot in twenty-five hundred years, management should act like it.

Twenty

The Most Valuable Asset

THERE IS A MUCH TO be said about the quality of a leader who knows exactly the right time to take a gamble at the risk of the people driving the machine forward. Throughout history, there are innumerable examples of leaders with the foresight to throw in the towel before an unfavorable occurrence became all too real. There are an equal number of examples of individuals who through characteristics, such as greed, vengeance, pride and careless disregard, led a group of people straight off a cliff and onto the jagged rocks below. In situations where a leader has the opportunity to predict an inevitable outcome, it is crucial the energy and focus shift from what could have been won to what can be salvaged in the moment.

At the onset of the year 1943, the world was fated to experience the bloodiest and most devastating two-year period in history. The German war machine under Adolf Hitler was grinding away against the Russian peasant legions in unimaginably large military engagements during the Siege of Leningrad and the Battle of Stalingrad. The Third Reich had delivered a catastrophic toll upon the people of Russia during these conflicts, and it was the exploitation of gruesomely harsh tactics, implemented by Joseph Stalin, which saw the Russian army capable of obtaining any application of resilience towards the German invasion. The enlistment of a peasant soldier class along with the implementation of Order Number 227 gave the Russian military the upper hand during the years long engagement with Germany. Order Number 227, also called "not one step back!" allowed Russian officers to execute any combatant retreating from battle without trial. This single ordinance turned off any human fear factor from the Russian military equation.

As the year 1943 continued, the Third Reich started to experience the impending doom that would follow some of the major losses experienced at the end of these two major battles. After Stalingrad was lost and the German military was in retreat, a great counteroffensive action was orchestrated on the eastern front during the Battle of Kursk. This single battle saw the largest armored clashes in the history of warfare. One of the final nails in the coffin for the Third Reich's eastern ambitions was the heavy losses inflicted upon the German war machine during the Battle of Kursk. Furthermore, also forcing the German top brass to experience the first major German Offensive in which German momentum was not allowed to break through an enemy line of defense. The Russians held back the aggressive push by the Germans once and for all. This in turn gave the Russian nation the continuous momentum to conclude the war for good. After the Siege of Leningrad was finally lifted and the final German offensive quelled, there was little stopping the complete destruction of the empire built by Hitler's Nazi Germany.

There was little to be said or done about the eventual downfall of Nazi Germany. From the West, the Allies were beginning to carry out Operation Overlord and the eventual liberation of France under German rule. Germany was going to experience a catastrophic defeat under the Russians, and yet the American and British liberation of France simply added an extra layer of impending defeat to the destruction of Hitler's Germany. It is in these moments that many leaders define the legacy for which the world will remember them, it is in times of great adversity that will define a leader as a victor or as a dismal failure. In either case, Hitler was a genocidal madman, but the opportunity to save the German people did present itself during the end of 1943. The world was exhausted from war, and no one could imagine or predict what an unconditional surrender of Germany at the end of 1943 could have meant for the future of the Europe. It is without a doubt the death toll brought upon the German people between the end of 1943, and the conclusion of the war in 1945 could have been moderately subdued. Hitler was only content on one conclusion, total victory or total death.

Once the war was a proven failure to the German people, questions began to arise to Hitler's capabilities to see Germany through the war without forcing the country to endure suicidal levels of engagement with the outside world. It was at this exact moment that many of the highest-ranking officials in Germany attempted to carry out the assassination of Adolf Hitler. After the assassination was a failure, Hitler became paranoid beyond comprehension and his evil trends began to be directed towards many of the German men and women he once had called allies. Hitler's passionate and evil madness, which had once been exploited by the German Nazi Party for unity, became the very enemy from within that would sign the final death note of the old-world German nation.

True leaders that wish to define themselves as saviors of a grand cause do so by labeling a risk that would present itself to the deliverance and execution of the positive cause within and without. Hitler had the opportunity to sense the opening in which the German people could have been saved from an invasion by Communist Russia. Once the Russians had entered the city of Berlin, the destruction that followed became all too apparent, and the outside world was able to witness a world subject to Communist Russian rule. There was little held back by the Russian soldiers during the invasion of Germany and of Berlin, mostly due to the violence by which the Russians had experienced under the hands of the Germans themselves. Reprisal for sinister actions was followed through by more violence by the invading Red Army, specifically towards the civilian population of Germany. While both sides fought to end the war their own way, it was the people along the entire eastern front that truly suffered the greatest. Genocide, extermination, rape and other war crimes were demonstrated by both sides of the war on the eastern front.

So, the risk was real and the consequences were obviously presented to Hitler. What actions prove his motivation to see through only complete and total victory at the expense of the German people? The proof stands within the actions taken by Hitler during the final two years of the war. One of Hitler's closest advisors was a man by the name of Albert Speer. Speer was an architect that had caught the eye of Hitler early on in his political career. Once the German war machine was turning, Speer had been given control of the entire national German armament production for the war effort. This role, as you could imagine, was crucial to the success Germany sought in the martial dominance of Eastern, Western Europe and Northern Africa.

During the year 1942 to 1943, there was an increase in German aircraft production by 51 percent, followed by another increase of 80 percent between the years 1943 and 1944. Between the years 1942 and 1943, there was an increase in German tank and armored vehicle production by 68 percent, followed by an additional increase of 51 percent between the years 1943 and 1944. Towards the end of the war, the production time for the workhorse submarine, the U-boat, was reduced from a one-year period to a two-month period. By halfway through 1944, there was enough military equipment to supply 270 German army divisions while there were only 150 army divisions in the field.

As we can see, the focus for Hitler and his top advisors was in stubbornly pursuing the mastery of production output during the final years of the war. After major losses, in some of largest and bloodiest conflicts in human history, there was little doubt that the Third Reich was walking towards a fast approaching cliff. The priority of Hitler's conquered Europe stayed absolute, and there was every effort put forth to ensure enough industry was engaged to see that the assets of war were supplied to the front lines. When it had become apparent that the manpower needed to field these armaments were in short supply, Hitler turned to old men and young children to fight battles during the invasion of Germany by the Russians, eventually leading to the Siege of Berlin, followed by the total collapse of old-world Germany and her people.

As was experienced by the German people under the Russian invasion between 1943 and 1945, little could have been done to refocus the attention of the Russian legions from total German annihilation, to one of peaceful annexation. Eastern Germany lost almost all identity with itself after the Russians took over in 1945. The culture, society and people of Eastern Germany were at risk of being lost, all while Hitler's war production quotas were prioritized and gained. While the number of armaments produced had reached record numbers, the German communities that held the people with the ability to wage Hitler's war had become desolate and barren.

There comes a point in all successful business organizations when similar decisions become a real stressful predicament for many aspiring leaders. When organizations are small and personable interaction with leadership is apparent, the disenfranchisement of the employee group is less likely to occur. As companies scale and grow, there begins to form an invisible wall between leadership and lower level employees. In many mid to large size organizations, the lowest tier employee would be lucky to have a seat at the annual CEO performance presentation, as an example.

This non-association makes it challenging for leadership to retain the perspective the people of the organization truly define the scope and nature of an organization by its scalable definition. There are very few investor pitches in the world in which a CEO brags about the number of computers, office chairs, desks and staplers a company may possess. Companies will define their scalable success based off income, funding availability and employee growth in most examples. People make the company a living and breathing entity.

If an organization were to ignore the people from all equations and pursue production mastery without taking into consideration the people's interests within the organization, the company's very premise will become obsolete. The scope of a business is defined by the culture and context of the people who are motivated to work day in and day out to see the organization progress. Unfortunately for many CEO's, there is little chance that computers will be obtaining the human habit of motivational drive and ambition anytime within the next century.

Twenty-one

To Prepare and To Act

THERE ARE TIMES IN history when the predicted outcome of an inevitable engagement may seem too great to overturn, when all of the world's forces are turned towards you with the predisposition to stop at nothing to see to your destruction assured. There are many examples in history of great men and women turning back superior forces and experiencing a risky gamble providing a moment of fruition, while all other factors were taking the other side in the bet. Action is what all of the epic displays of storytelling have convinced us to embrace when times appear destitute or chances appear grim. The ability to act with diligent and aggressive execution is what our movies, novels and entertainment have given as the answer to all uphill battles. An individual who takes the initiative during a window of opportunity to strike when the enemy is least expecting is what our human culture to this point has convinced us as the single most important component of achieving success against all odds. There are very few times, though, when the glory of a legendary achievement is depicted with the gritty, rudimentary and unforgiving necessity that all stories are absolutely dependent upon embracing.

In the world of 218 B.C., there were many major and subtle differences to our world today. One consistency between the two was obvious; that all people respected results garnered by actions above all else. Carthaginian generals during the Punic Wars against Rome lead vast armies to glory, loss and death. The fertile lands in Sicily were lost to the Romans during the early Punic Wars, and through victories in Italy, the Roman Empire started to truly take shape as the dominant player in the Mediterranean.

Rome had a massive navy, elite infantry, the strongest cavalry and ambition from the leadership and people alike. If there was an intimidating force in the world, it was Roman legions marching through your lands with a wake of subjugation, enslavement and morbid justice.

The Carthaginian empire was strong to say the least. Their dominance in the Western Mediterranean had been slowly dwindling since the onset of the Punic Wars with the eventual loss of crucial lands in Sicily, Corsica and Sardinia. Rome had subjugated large portions of Carthaginian land and worst of all, had seen the death of the greatest Carthaginian general of the era, Hamilcar Barca. Peace did not last long after the First Punic War, and the Carthaginians and Romans were at it again by 218 B.C. This time, the son of Hamilcar, Hannibal Barca, obtained control of the Carthaginian legions of infantry, cavalry and war elephants.

When it came to pitched battles against the Roman legions, the Carthaginians were at a severe disadvantage. Roman cavalry and infantry were superior to Carthaginian, and direct engagements typically would swing in the favor of Roman might of arms. Romans were also the greatest siege artists in the world and could sack city after city with elaborate designs far outside the intellect and abilities of other nations. Carthaginian territory held in the Iberian Peninsula was fragile to say the least. Rome knew this and wanted to expressly pursue these opportunities for ever growing dominance in the west. Finally, the Roman Navy was far superior in might when compared to that of the Carthaginians. Any elongated naval conflicts would not bode well for Carthage landing craft. The legions under Hannibal were truly at a disadvantage when pursuing the Second Punic War with Rome.

Any invasion of lands lost prior to the Romans would have been met with a timely defeat by the armies of Rome. Hannibal had to make some fast and wise decisions followed by swift and direct execution if Carthage was to continue to stake claim in the Western Mediterranean for years to come. Hannibal had decided to take the route of action that had never been achieved by any large-scale army in history up to this point in time. Hannibal through pure tactical genius had lead his army of 100,000 men around the Roman legions, who were chasing him, in the Iberian

Peninsula, and up through Southern Gaul to the outside foot of the Alps. It was then that Hannibal was set to achieve one of the greatest military maneuvers of all time, leading tens of thousands of men, horses, elephants and supplies through tight, narrow, steep and cold passes through the Alps.

Why was it that Hannibal had decided to take this approach, to cross the Alps with thousands of native African men and cavalry accompanied with elephants bred for war? What lead him to take such an action? Was it simply a window of opportunity that was granted at a moment's notice, Hannibal's ability to simply act upon such an opportunity being the sole component of success? The story dives way deeper here, more so than any entertainment mechanism would ever be willing to elaborate upon. Hannibal had to label the window of opportunity by planning 20 steps ahead and following through with subtle acts of calculated preparation in order to even understand whether or not a window of opportunity was even plausible.

First, there was the issue of reaching the Alps. There were numerous bridges well defended by Roman troops and Gaelic Mercenaries. In order to do so without losing excessive troops in costly battles before ever reaching the Alps, manual river crossings were planned and staged to transfer everything from horses and supplies, to even elephants across ferry's.

Also, there was the ever-present risk that the Roman legions would catch up with Hannibal's assembled army. Any pitched battle would be costly and would by far eliminate any chance of an invasion force passing through the Alps with enough bodies to pose a threat on the other side. Hannibal directed his brothers to march with men in varying directions in order to dislodge pursuing Roman troops. These tactics allowed the main force under Hannibal to remain strong as the force neared the foothills of the Alps.

Hannibal knew that there was no way of crossing the Alps unhindered by Gaelic Barbarians throughout the narrow passes when soldiers would be walking single file for long lengths of time. Also, the routes of least resistance and the most optimum paths to take would have been known by the local tribes better than anyone else. The Gaul's in the south possessed many lands on the other side of the Alps as well. An alliance with these groups would have provided Hannibal with needed rest and an advantageous spot to organize and plan raids against Roman territory. Envoys were sent to Gaelic leaders throughout the region to establish commonality between the parties against the Romans. Knowledge was gathered, and pacts were established. Finally, a large clearing was labeled as the final conclusive place for which Hannibal was determined to see his army gather after spending exhausting weeks crossing dangerous mountain passes.

Furthermore, Carthaginian scouts were sent ahead of the main army in order to ensure that surprises were not in store for the marching armies under Hannibal. These scouts would map potential routes, locate hostile tribes and would help to ensure that the Romans were never aware of the invasion force making its way through the mountains. There is little doubt that Hannibal, as a leader, would have been blind without the use of scouts throughout the risky excursion into the Alps.

It is hard to imagine Hannibal taking the trek into the dangerous mountain passes of the barbarian infested Alps without having spent a long and necessary amount of time in the planning phases. The firsthand accounts of the march through the Alps label a total count of sixteen days having been needed to march the army through the mountains. Once Hannibal had reached mainland Italy on the other side, only 6,000 fighting men survived the experience. This was enough to cause a massive breach in the security of the Roman interior. Hannibal and his troops went on to sack, pillage and raid the rich inland of Roman rule. With assistance from the Gaul's, Hannibal posed a real issue to the Roman generals, whom had just been completely outmaneuvered. While the instability and destruction caused by Hannibal during this invasion was seen as a great victory, there was never any hope in actually continuing through with the conquering of Rome itself. Hannibal ended his invasion having accomplished one of the greatest military feats of all time, even to this day, against all odds and logic.

It is easy to imagine what modern media's depiction of Hannibal's march through the Alps would or could look like. It would most likely be three hours of soldiers marching through mountains, dealing with barbarians and eventually pillaging Roman plebeians. The drama that would unfold would be of epic proportion and yet would do an absolute injustice to the level of complexity that Hannibal had invested into the excursion in the first place. The amount of planning and organization that had occurred behind the scenes in preparation for the actual action is materially significant to the premise of the action itself. It is difficult to imagine, but not hard to admit, there must have been weeks and months of preparation time spent in just organizing the supply carts, which would see the tens of thousands of men through the Alps.

While the glory of the action is often the focal point in all immersive storytelling by modern media, glory is not won with action alone. This rings just as true within the organizational goals and energies of a modern entrepreneurial venture. It is one thing to have an idea and to take action upon said idea, yet it is a wise person who seeks planning through all stages of a business engagement. Before investing resources, such as money and time, into an idea with action, set tiers of planning in order to prepare you and your business for the trials ahead. There is little to no doubt that while glory is obtained through immediate action, there will be no glory to be had if the action itself is not backed up with a competent strategy and a worthwhile plan.

Twenty-two

Against All Odds

THERE ARE GOING TO be decisions during the course of your business that will define the opportunities that have the potential to originate. All business ventures require windows of opportunity in order to achieve a long-sought objective, and there are no exceptions to this rule. When hunting for those opportunities, the keys to success derive from an ability to think and act both creatively and objectively within the blink of an eye. It may seem difficult to visualize a scenario in which such qualities play hand in hand, but the facts show that an unwillingness to embrace the very chaos that will thrust opportunities in your path, at immense risk, is the first nail in the coffin of your already failed business.

There was at one moment in history a young country waging an uphill battle against the political, social and economic framework of the age. In reality, the concepts laid by the founders of this nation were so revolutionary that it has cost hundreds of years of constant war to keep the ideologies pure and the direction of the state unbroken. There are few better examples of subversive and insurrectionary action than the establishment and early melioration of The United States of America. This nation in its infancy is truly a story of arduous exploration that every aspiring individual should know to learn.

In 1801, the United States was very much a different nation than the one we can call home today. In fact, it is not that hard to argue that the nation was in a state of constant debate as to the path for which it should walk. It is also an easy theory to put forth that the name 'United States' was about as absurd as it was ideological.

There was more nationalism within each state entity than there was at the federal level. In fact, the political partisanship was exactly that, federalist versus democratic-republicans—the central government argument versus state independence. To say that unity within the union at that time was rare is like stating that humans need water to drink.

There were persistent debates at the federal, state and dinner table level regarding the role of the national government within a constitutionally free republic. On one side, there were individuals who believed a strong central government will allow for a more competitive advantage when dealing with the world powers in Europe, and individuals across the young country believed this would only lead to another form of tyrannical monarchy, for which the country had just violently escaped.

When Thomas Jefferson was elected president in 1801, the nation's core problems stemmed far beyond the debate around the role of central government within the functions of economics, politics and foreign affairs. The War for Independence, the establishment of the first government, the printing of both federal and state currency and numerous other issues facing a developing nation had left the country in vast debt.

The nation had very little in terms of amiable relations with Europe besides France, and at the time this was actually a very detrimental friendship from the perspective of the other established powerhouses. France under Napoleon was currently besieging Europe and causing an era of war and turmoil of the likes that have never been seen before then and would never be seen again until the era of the world wars. France was a republic ruled by a self-appointed monarch, and the rest of Europe saw republicanism as a threat beyond that of any plague, famine or religious extremism. The United States was not only a baby in influence and power when compared to the monarchies of Europe, it was also a beacon of republican light at the denunciation of European hegemony.

Finally, there was the status of foreign trade with the European nations willing to make monetary gain off the recently lost British colony. This was a very opportunistic position the United States had taken great measures to ensure remain open after the British Empire was no longer overseeing U.S. merchant fleets in foreign waters. Once the U.S. rebelled against the British, the nation lost protection from pirates commonly present within the Mediterranean, most notably the Islamic Barbary States of North Africa. Trade with Europe was crucial for the young nation to develop internally, prevent future British incursion and to pursue continued westward expansion. With the loss of any status of protection by a European power, the United States was forced to negotiate on its own behalf with the pirates of the Barbary States in order to protect ships, trade goods and of course, the sailors themselves from enslavement.

When U.S. merchant ships were continuing to experience pirate raids from the Barbary States, there became a very prominent discussion within Thomas Jefferson's cabinet regarding how to handle this problem. At the time, the U.S. Navy was nonexistent, and with the current debt the young nation was in, it was almost impossible to deploy congress for any assistance in the manner. The U.S. was also at a point in which losing trading capabilities in the Mediterranean would have further dismantled the economic progress and foreign affinity earned to this point. The United States under Thomas Jefferson faced an extremely imperative and decisive decision to make in regards to how it would handle protecting their foreign merchant ships from attacks by the Barbary States. A wrong decision regarding this specific issue could have meant short work of economic potential and the death of the validity the United States was able to protect itself from more established world powers.

The options were laid as followed: build a Navy to protect our merchant fleets in the Mediterranean. This was extremely risky because of cost, it would retract investment into westward expansion and it would also display a hostile stance against already trigger-happy European powers. There was the option of bribing and paying monetary tributes to the North African states in return for ceased hostilities. This was expensive, unstable and uniformly difficult due to the fact that the Barbary States consisted of four completely independent kingdoms. Also, there was the option to do nothing and to continue to allow sailors and merchantmen to fair hostile waters at the hope of losing less than it would cost to enact the other two options. This was not only risky and potentially of higher cost than the first two options, but also was immensely unbecoming of a nation taking pride in establishing the human birthright and had just fought a war over the still newly enacted Constitution of the United States.

As one could imagine, the decision to protect American interests overseas couldn't have come at a worse time. The situation, in many ways, resembles the modern entrepreneurial venture in the 21st century—young and fragile startup with limited or no resources followed by very little external support. The opportunity for success is pitiful compared to the chances for failure. Thomas Jefferson's decisive moment captures one of the crucial components that all young organizations face. Furthermore, the window of opportunity only shows itself briefly and a lot of times is disguised behind a mask of risk, cost and detrimental backlash. There are few entrepreneurships that have experienced eras of success without fighting a lopsided battle, due to the slim and rare chance for success. One must always weigh all options, label the most preferential opportunity, assess an affinity for risk and eventually take the plunge if an entrepreneurship is ever going to be destined for greatness. One simply cannot stumble into success, it is earned through fearless advancement while staring directly into the eyes of overwhelming circumstances and intimidating forces.

The route Thomas Jefferson took at first was bribing and pledging tribute to each individual Barbary State faction. This cost the U.S. vast sums of money during a time of financial hardship and central instability. Some accounts reference one tenth of total U.S. revenue was pledged to the Barbary States for cessation of pirate activity. This pact between some of the Barbary State factions was short-lived, tribute became increasingly demanded and the burden of the U.S. to continue to pay such steep sums of money began to weigh heavily on the young nation. Eventually, a more aggressive action was required, and Thomas Jefferson set out establishing the U.S. Navy.

Once enough ships were commissioned, the first Naval offensive action was undertaken in which multiple U.S. warships were deployed into the Mediterranean in order to defend the U.S. merchant fleets in the region. It was not long before an all-out war was underway between the U.S. Navy and the Barbary States. Ships were destroyed, including the USS Philadelphia, by its own U.S. Marines, after it was mistakenly grounded and commandeered by the enemy. The city of Derna was captured by the U.S. and stands as the first foreign city ever conquered by the U.S. Eventually, America had dealt a toll on the Barbary State factions and in turn had negotiated a peace treaty. In exchange for sixty thousand U.S. dollars, the Barbary States were forced to return all American prisoners and cease hostilities against U.S. ships in the Mediterranean. It was the first offensive conflict engaged in by the U.S., and it was a great victory for the aspiring nation both in the eyes of the people of the United States and in the eyes of the monarchies of Europe, who had every intention of believing a peasant state could in no way succeed in this world.

With every young aspiring venture comes decisive moments. I will say most ventures fail because of an inability to either move past difficult moments or the loss of an affinity to pursue risk. If you as an entrepreneur ever want to amount to anything, the moment when you decide to hang up on your business because you view a necessary set of actions as all inevitable losing battles, is the day you will be guaranteed to lose your business. All ventures face uphill battles, and all ventures face moments of ill-wanted and inevitable loss. These are the moments within the course of your business in which you must push through. Perhaps the precursor of a major loss may wind up leading to a window of opportunity all because you had decided to take the risk, incur the cost and experience the dawn of a new day.

Twenty-three

The Balance of Leadership

THE QUESTION, "How do we define leadership?" begins and ends with the character of the person giving the answer. There are very few people in the world that can claim to have the right combination of talents, traits, exposures and weaknesses to align with the proper vision of a true leader. It is easy to conclude the reason these combinations are so rare within our world is most likely because the true leader personification is a rarer form than that of the follower component. When a true leader emerges from the chaos of human culture, it is the followers that define the leader's capability to exercise such leadership qualities. If all of these mechanisms are in place, the right leader at the right time in history has the propensity to redefine the world around us.

Different leadership styles tend to define the leader as an individual. There have been entire libraries of books written about defining leadership as an item to be poked and prodded. True leadership is obtained through direct experience within the context of the nature of leadership itself. This always takes form in the real world with hands on exposure, often leading to bloody noses and scuffed emotions. It is never learned through the pages of a textbook. That is why we embrace history as our guide through the textbook exposure of leadership as a character. To tell a story of the men and women leaders of our past is to both bring their exploits to the light while also embedding their lives within our own. One such leader, a man of the greatest caliber of men, was everything that we as aspiring leaders within the entrepreneurial, government, military, entertainment or social realms of the high tech 21st century could ever hope to embody.

In 1898, there was a war in the Caribbean where the emerging American empire fought against the dissolving Spanish empire. The American public despised the colonial Spanish rule so close to the American border, and Cuban independence was a top priority for the emerging world power. Theodore Roosevelt was in every way the leader within the hearts of men under his command. One great example was during the Battle of San Juan Heights when the "Rough Riders" regiment of ambitious cavalrymen led an assault on foot up a defended position on an elevated hill. While his men were trudging up the hill, Roosevelt was on his horse, riding up and down the hill at great risk to his own person to encourage bravery within his men. One of the best methods of displaying leadership among followers is inspiring fortitude within others by displaying strength of will and courage within oneself.

A few years later, Theodore Roosevelt was given the opportunity to run for vice president on a ticket with William McKinley, who at the time was a major proponent for progressive movement and American imperialism. McKinley, as a proponent of American imperialism, was known for his annexation of Hawaii and the procurement of Puerto Rico, Guam and the Philippines. One evening, within a year after the election for his second term as president, McKinley was shot in a receiving line by a young anarchist who had been self-motivated and reaffirmed in his anarchist mentality by some very iconic individuals of the era, such as Emma Goldman. When McKinley was shot, the role of president fell into the hands of Theodore Roosevelt. Without any hesitation, Roosevelt was steadfast in his eagerness and fervor in taking on such a tremendous responsibility. The men and women in America rallied around his persona in the wake of such catastrophe, which in every way symbolizes the role a true leader must exemplify when the time comes to lift the world on one's shoulders.

Leaders think not only of themselves, but also of every component that fits within the makeup of their leadership character. There are many stories that can define Roosevelt as both a man of great character and of great universal thinking when he demonstrated his most long lasting legacy from his presidential years. Theodore's character had always been categorized by his love for the outdoors and the heart he had for outdoor excursions into the American wilderness. This is why, to the protest of many Americans of the day, he laid out the national park system in order to preserve one of the greatest assets America has to offer; natural serenity. This was an era of heavy industry, oil booms and massive deforestation. To the disgust of many growing industrial tycoons of the age, Roosevelt predicted and acted upon his belief that the national park system was a crucial component to the American way of life. Leaders act upon their foresight and beliefs with unapologetic rigor to the benefit of those that may not have the same viewpoint at the time.

The genuine and humble tendencies of a leader in action will demonstrate both short-term consistency and long-term dependability to followers seeking these qualities, which tend to be all people. Genuine affinity is proven by following through with promises, such as the time Theodore Roosevelt had made a vow to seek re-election in 1904 for the 1908 race. When 1908 came, he had become exhausted by almost two full terms of presidential participation. To his reluctance, Theodore Roosevelt ran for another term as president to hold true to his genuine character. Humble tendencies are proven by an embrace of many of the little things in life all people live to love. Roosevelt always made time for his family and children, even during times of important state matters. This humble stance always found ways of driving respect and admiration from the men and women who sought his leadership.

Continuous learning is one of the most crucial components of any thoughtful leader's arsenal of influence. To admit that we as individuals, leaders or not, must how to the graces of educational enrichment at all points within a career is absolutely crucial to your ability to be a competent and effective person. Theodore Roosevelt was known for always reading books that sparked his curiosity, whether they be relevant to the occasion or not. He had books hidden in places for which he frequently found himself waiting. His pursuit of knowledge across all paths of study was legendary to his persona and the attitude his followers shared of his wisdom. Roosevelt believed wholeheartedly that a leader who doesn't consistently learn new information has no new lessons to teach.

In today's media, you always see the same types of political leaders. Ones that communicate and work well with their friends, all while feuding with the opposition. This forms a short-sighted perspective. The 21st century media opinion of the modern consumer is almost of absolute short-sightedness and often paves a road of dissidence toward an opposite stance. From an actual productivity standpoint, there is little to nothing to gain from only working with individuals who are on your side of an argument. Theodore Roosevelt knew this and lived this throughout his political career. When he was governor of New York, he often communicated and worked alongside members of the opposing side. Throughout Roosevelt's career he made frequent maneuvers to seek out and meet with people whom his allies would fear would always seek to take advantage of their team's side. Roosevelt as a powerful leader feared this also and yet pursued consistent communication with the opposition in order to enact a philosophy of action above all else.

Furthermore, Theodore Roosevelt was an effective leader because he himself ensured the caliber of people closest to himself would perform to a higher degree of success than what he was able to deliver. The people Roosevelt surrounded himself with were strong, ambitious, intelligent and all around solid people of character. Some of the most legendary figures of his era were people whom Roosevelt sought to embrace. Elihu Root was given the title of Secretary of State, and among other things, was one of the most prestigious individuals to have ever shared the title. Other individuals whom Roosevelt put into place around himself in key roles were William Howard Taft, Gifford Pinchot and Oliver Wendell Holmes Jr. The ambitious characters we have in our lives speak leagues around the character we try to embody as we pursue ambitions. Other outside forces will always judge, there will always be individuals seeking to impede and yet, if you are careful with your planning, the individuals on your team can counter any negative play by an opponent.

Twenty-four

The Definition of Success

IMAGINE A WORLD in which lawlessness, barbarism and survival instinct were a practical reality all while justice, civility and comfort were dreams of the gods. The lives of people 2100 years ago could be exemplified within an individual's fight or flight mentality, without break. The chances were good that an invading barbarian tribe would sack the farmstead, steal the women, steal the cattle, steal the children and leave you clinging to suicide as a rescue from pure helplessness. To take up arms in groups was the only chance a single individual had to protect one's life and the lives of one's families. This literal world is easily the purest form of true barbaric competition, some 2100 years ago. Pure capitalist competition with blood as capital and surviving to next year as your profit motive. This was absolutely the case across all of the known world, until of course when the Roman Republic, through the will of the Roman people, spread its talons and subjected the entire world from Asia minor and North Africa to Southern and Western Europe. Julius Caesar was beyond our imagining of the definition of success some 2100 years ago.

Caesar was by no means born to a poor family, this is not a rags to riches story, and his ambition was truly abundant. He had married into a noble family in order to further his potential influence across the leagues of the ruling classes of Rome. The power-hungry ruler of Rome at the time, Sulla, had taken a tyrannical approach at physically capturing power in Rome, which made young aspiring men like Caesar an enemy of the tyrant. Caesar therefore spent time in the military, venturing east to see the world from the eyes of a legionnaire. Upon the death of Sulla,

Caesar returned to Rome with the intention of pursuing a political career within the Republic of Rome. During his early years as a power seeker, he successfully fought in a few campaigns to win him subtle renown within the nobility of Rome. One particular noble, Pompey, took excessive interest in Caesar, going as far as enlisting him as a low level political aid.

Pompey had ambition with the wealth and resources to match. His rise within the republican bureaucracy of Rome speaks leagues about the type of man Pompey was. Under Pompey, Caesar was able to advance quickly through the ranks of Roman rule. Eventually, Caesar was granted governorship of the Iberian Peninsula and was risen to the prestigious rank of Consul. Consul was the highest position a politician could aspire to achieve under the Roman Republic and there were only two seats available within the republic every year. Caesar's alliance with Pompey was an astute maneuver for Caesar and had cemented his place within the highest rulers of the Roman Republic at that time. It should be stated that Rome was, at this time, entirely ruled as a republic. Laws and political pursuits were driven through different bodies of political leaders of the plebeian council, made up of commoners, and also the aristocratic senate, made up of patricians. With the complexity of the Roman Republic came great strength to the common Roman citizen but also left an opportunity for one smart enough to exploit.

Caesar needed an opportunity to leap away from dependence on Pompey's power for continued ascension. Therefore, he pursued a relationship with an extremely wealthy general, Crassus, whom gave Caesar the financial and political backing to continue his pursuit of power and success. In order to quell unrest from Pompey at this obvious display of rivalry, Caesar negotiated an alliance between the three parties in order to secure the powerful position he had won for himself. This alliance split Rome politically in a three-way competition for influence. It was Caesar who was able to secure one of the more chaotic regions as his governorship, Gaul, while the other two men held positions in more secure regions of the empire. It was this opportunity for glory that gave Caesar the catalyst he needed on the road to continued glory.

When Julius Caesar marched his legions into Roman occupied Gaul for the first time, the intent was never to settle for governing the already maintained roman territories. Caesar set out drawing lines in the sand between the Gallic tribes who were willing to ally themselves with the Roman Empire and the Gallic tribes who would need to be removed. The Senate and people of Rome were not necessarily in line with Caesar's ambitions until there was the risk of increased migration of the Helvetii, a very large mountain based Gallic people who sought to settle in more fertile lands east of the Alps.

Caesar could not let this migration happen, so therefore used it as the premise he needed in order to declare war upon the Helvetii. The Roman legions butchered and enslaved many of these people, starting a journey of conquest through Western Europe that would see the subjection of hundreds of thousands of Gallic people. Victory after victory pushed Caesar and his legions onward. Caesar's inspiring presence on the battlefield alongside his troops inspired his legions with immense confidence, and Caesar's legendary status grew with every passing day.

When a standing advantage was acquired against the Gaul in today's France, Caesar saw his next course laid out in front of him—the sea between mainland Europe and Britain. Caesar knew being the first Roman to conquer the British Isle would give him immense prestige in Rome, therefore he amassed his legions and sailed across the channel to set foot on Britain. At first, there was intense conflict during the invasions with victory handed to the Romans. Once Caesar crossed the channel a second time, he was greeted with obedience and domination over the people of southern Britain. Caesar had achieved his goal of turning Britain into a Roman territory, which in turn added a notch on his belt of legendary victories.

After it had become status quo of Roman occupation of Gallic tribes within Western Europe, an uprising occurred by some of the largest and most powerful Gaul. For the first time ever, the Roman empire and Caesar faced a unified threat of a single Gaul nation at their doorstep. Caesar rallied the legions of Rome and set forth to stop, once and for all, the Gaul threat to Rome. In what is known as Caesar's greatest military achievement, through cunning and brutal tactics he laid siege to Gaul with all of the might of the Roman Republic. The engineering and military sophistication of Rome was fully leveraged by Caesar during this campaign. Add this with Caesar's merciless handling of the Gaul aggressors and Caesar supplanted himself in the history books as one of the most accomplished and brutal warlords of all time. Vercingetorix, the Gallic warlord who was responsible for leading the unified Gallic tribes against Rome, was eventually captured and executed in Rome to supplant Caesar as an almost divine figure of power in the eyes of the Roman people.

After the conquest of Gaul was complete and the stabilization of the Western empire was assured, Caesar returned to Rome not as a passive general but as a conqueror of Rome's enemies and of Rome itself. His once strong alliances with Pompey and other Roman nobles were pushed to the point of breaking, starting a civil war within the highest classes of Rome. Due to Caesar's military might and aggressive nature, he pushed Pompey out of Italy eventually leading to his demise in the Egyptian province. After Caesar's enemies within the nobility had been quelled, he aligned himself with Cleopatra, the divine leader of Egypt, and they had a son together. This maneuver for power meant Caesar saw himself as above the confinements of the Republic for which all prior Roman leaders had been restricted by. When he came back to Rome, he did so as a dictator and was given complete control over the workings of the now established Roman Empire.

His time as a dictator was rich in executive decisions that saw the structure of Rome maneuver into the favor of the people of Rome, rather than the noble ruling classes. He sustained his power by ensuring his allies received preferential treatment within the senate and that honors, title and coins all bore his name. While his popularity with the masses grew to levels of immense influence, his rapport with the senate had become stretched and thin. Caesar was the first Roman dictator in half a millennium; there were few amiable attitudes in the ruling classes to continue to support a monarchy within Rome.

Caesar seldom made mistakes during his ascension to power within Rome. He was quick to judge and fast to action. Often, he would finish a job completely, and rarely did he leave room for opportunities of insurrection within the people that remained after his sword arm fell. There was one very impactful mistake made by Julius Caesar during the conclusion of the civil war, which would write his doom. When Pompey had rebelled against Caesar's aggressive occupation of Rome, he took with him a number of Caesar's prior allies whom had had enough of the power-hungry dictator. Marcus Brutus and Gaius Cassius Longinus had maintained the trust of Caesar even though they had sided with Pompey during the revolt against Caesar. After the civil war had ended and Pompey was dead, Brutus and Cassius obtained favor again with Caesar. Both were appointed to the senate with the support of Caesar himself. These two men, in the position that they were in and their loyalties judged directly by Caesar himself, were the cancer within Caesar's Rome.

It wasn't long after Caesar had claimed rule over Rome that he was assassinated by the senate. Caesar was lead to the senate floor, was surrounded and stabbed to death by a majority of the senators present who all wanted to be a part of the coup against the enemy of the Roman Republic. This action would cement Caesar as a martyr and a legend, leading to his rise as a divine figure within pagan Rome. It wasn't until Caesar's great-grandnephew Octavian, who took the name Caesar Augustus, enabled a military offensive against the Roman Republic and saw to the permanent rise of the Roman Empire under the Caesars.

Caesar's actions, victories and his eventual downfall has been the subject matter of countless books throughout the ages of human civilization. There have been few individuals within the history of humankind that represent the purest form of established success leading to revolutionary influence. Caesar was a man with the gift for seeing through to victory against all odds and turning any counter-action into an action in his favor. His ultimate strength was his ability to lead the subordinate masses against his enemies in all things. There were few leaders who have demonstrated a greater fortitude for focusing on enhancing prestige from the mindset of the population of citizens, all while treating the ruling noble class solely as an instrument of his own volition.

While Caesar climbed the ladder of his own success to greater and greater achievements, he had climbed onto the backs of numerous allies, including the citizenry and the soldier classes of Rome. Once at the top few rungs of the ladder, he had chosen to place into power a few hidden enemies. His trust in a few weak men lead to his assassination. His faith in his own ability, power and influence lead to his comfort and sense of immunity. His luxury at having the ability to choose the influencers around himself lead to his comfort in picking some of the weakest links in the chain in positions of power around himself. If you fall from the top rung of the ladder, it is the furthest fall one can take.

Twenty-five

A Legendary Idea

LEGENDARY IDEAS ARE easy to pick out of the mix with hindsight. In history, there have been numerous thoughts that have turned into truly magnificent displays of what the human collective is capable of. Go to your nearest library, and you will spend the rest of your life reading about legendary accomplishments that have spurned from the minds of legendary people. The truth of the matter though is that today, what we consider to be legendary thought is incorrectly harnessed and given poor long-term trajectory towards success, whether it be a grand new mobile app, a brilliant start-up concept with a large propensity for first mover status, or the average graphic designer who has just re-invented the way the design industry could approach a common flaw. Legendary thought today is often viewed as immediately profitable. This is by far the greatest disservice that we today have become accustomed to when internalizing legendary thought.

There was once a time when the worlds of the earth were truly that; independent groups of people with no clue of the other side of a vast desert or the distant trek through a climbing mountain range. Humans in history have had to give it their everything in order to traverse the Earth, much like the effort that we today now need in order to be required to fix the limitless problems of our society. Problems are the most advantageous pursuit if you have a profit motive. This fact is a capitalist basic principle; fix a problem, find clients and earn. In the era of our ancestors, the problems of the age were an ocean of unknowns about the alien humans around our homes. This problem was solved and it took legendary ideas, legendary action, and a few millenniums worth of people.

When we sit in our classrooms as children learning about the world, there is one interesting fact about schooling of the 21st century that holds a consistency. A simple few words in the modern school curriculum can be the only requirements to embrace some of humanity's greatest achievements. The story of The Silk Road between ancient China and the west is perhaps the greatest example of a simple few words in modern schools. The story of The Silk Road holds with it the weight of our world. A hungry entrepreneur studying the legendary action required to build such a concept will better understand his or her place within the context of how legendary ideas become a reality.

First and foremost, in order for a legendary idea to become even plausible is the desire to venture forth. The earliest people in China were at a pinnacle point within their consolidation of power under the Han dynasty, after generations of war and turmoil, when continued movement westward became a possibility. A man by the name of Zhang Qian was ordered to venture into unknown western regions the Chinese had never explored, nor had any idea of what could be beyond the desert that lay to the west. The Xiongnu were an enemy of the Han dynasty. Their rise to power and conquering of the region west of China made it clear to the Chinese that another world beyond their own did exist. Once the Xiongnu were conquered, and after a truly epic lifelong journey into hostile lands, Zhang Qian came back to the Emperor Wu of the Han. The simple desire to reach beyond had within a moment made it clear to the Chinese that a vast world of kingdoms existed on this plane. A desire to grow and learn started The Silk Road out of China.

Once the world opened up to the Chinese in the 2nd century B.C., the roads that had once been paved by Alexander the Great were within the eyes of the Chinese Emperors. The only way the idea of exploration and profit exploitation could have become a reality was if an infrastructure was prepared in order to sustain the idea past the innumerable hurdles of the coming decades and centuries. Through efforts by the Han dynasty; consistent markings, roads, postal stations, relays and the ability to send messengers across the length of the known road were the hard-won components to the routes success.

In today's era of instant gratification, the hard truths that are the day in and day out labors of our trade are often played down. The cruel reality that many of us often forget is infrastructure is always necessary for scalability, and scalability is the only way for a legendary idea to become a tangible product. If it means spending months in a classroom to learn a skill or years in front of a computer to revise an initiative, no epic victory was ever won through minimum effort of practical application.

It is a great thing to have built a marvelous infrastructure accredited to a desire of mastery over a given challenge among the world. It is another to sell it to the world that ignorantly and stubbornly does not want to believe that the idea is needed. It is a truth that human culture has always and will always struggle with changing winds. This was no different for the men and women who traversed the chaos of The Silk Road.

At the time, China had a society that was of a complete different world compared to the rest of civilization at that time. Almost in pure isolation, the nation of China under the Han Dynasty was a collection of extremely powerful ruling factions, many of which would have in their own right rivaled many of the wealthiest factions in the west. The market in China was a truly legendary opportunity for trade exploitation. It took centuries before other global markets were confident enough to invest similar resources into The Silk Road compared to the Chinese. Factions, such as the Greeks, Syrians, Romans, Indians, Arabs, Parthians and many other groups, over time had to subject themselves to the enticing riches that The Silk Road had to offer. This is no different in fact to the 21st century start-ups having to view their own consumer markets with a motivation to bite at the idea.

Ultimately, when we sum up the development of The Silk Road into a modern business context, many parallels define the nature and task of your own legendary idea. The ultimate key to success, after having labeled the steps one must take to turn a legendary idea into a legendary conclusion, is through legendary action. These key moments of action paired with immense patience represent The Silk Road and the legendary actions required to achieve a level of success worthy of the classroom history books of today, no matter the unfortunate brevity.

Twenty-six

Unaccountability, Chaos and Retribution

THERE ARE LIMITLESS examples about elements of chaos within our surrounding society— businesses make it a point of stamping it out and turning a profit. The chaos inherent within our culture derive market potential, all while organizational chaos can and will inhibit production.

There was a baby born of a king whom had no other male heirs. The Crown Prince Sado of Korea was this baby and born he was among wealth, power and presence. At this time, the Korean peninsula was not without its problems, but the ruling family lived a life of utter concealment from the trials and tribulations of the common people. Sado was raised with education, martial training, full escort and the freedom to do as he wished. It was only his father, the king, whom held control over Prince Sado. The King Yeongjo was quick to anger and even faster to rage with his son. In fact, the very sight of Sado to the King had made him uncomfortable.

Sado always behaved well when the time was absolutely necessary, always dictated to by his father during times of official appearances. Outside of view from his father, the Crown Prince took to his own mental illnesses in order to create an era of hell for the people in his company. Women were raped and murdered. Men were murdered and extremities put on show before servants. If you were a woman of lower birth from the prince himself, pretty much only his sisters were of equal birth, you had to submit or would be outright raped and murdered. If you were in court or presided over the ruling family, you were at risk of death, disfigurement and worse. Sado had no accountability except to his father whom found him detestable yet necessary to uphold his family thrown.

It wasn't long before the Crown Prince had become more reckless and more careless in his attempts at deplorable and chaotic behavior. The Crown Prince in many ways represents pure unaccountability, which in turn will lead to internal chaos over the presiding "team" or "community" of people. In King Yeongjo's position, there was nothing that could have been done to stop the Crown Prince. To the people in the kingdom, the prince was divine. It wasn't until the chaos became too strong for the other people involved to bear any longer that steps were taken to eliminate the problem. If the setting derives unaccountability, and the prince is considered chaos, then only community retribution is capable of eliminating the continued threat. If no accountability exists, chaos is allowed to control the lives of the team until retribution happens or the team allows itself to be destroyed. Chaos inhibits perceived production; random acts of violence and depravity was the Crown Prince's tools of wielding chaos in an unaccountable environment.

After it had become known that not even the prince's own sisters were safe around the prince, the king took action. This action was taken only because the chaos had become far too great for the community to bear. The very fabric of the organization was at risk, King Yeongjo took action and enacted retribution to the Crown Prince Sado. Ensuring the king took precaution to not dismantle his divinity, he commanded Prince Sado to climb inside of a rice box. The box was locked, and the prince kept in there until he died. Retribution was enacted, the chaos eliminated. King Yeongjo and his kingdom of people were spared and eventually achieved their goal to become a well-respected ruling house that commanded great respect for their strict Confucian principles.

So now the question is asked, how does this remotely have anything to do with modern day capitalist theory? The truth of the matter, a lot. When taken into the context of how a productive environment is the single most important component in any business, chaos is by all means the antecedent to productive environments. Chaos by itself is usually quelled through QA and other assurance practices. When accountability is lost in a shuffle or caused by stagnation of any kind within the organization, chaos will eventually preside for longer than desired. The degrees of variation and severity of the chaos are as infinite as the actions themselves for which causes chaos to loom its ugly head.

If a president of a company receives a contract that no matter how the company performs in the next year, the president is guaranteed a 100% salary bonus, in what ways is the president accountable? Chaos looms when the president's lazy attitude takes the driver seat during a pressed time to hit quota. If an employee is allowed to punch his or her own time card, the chances for random interpretations of "time worked" will become unreliable, spilling into years of lost earnings for both employee and employer. If an artist in agency is given a project with no expedient deadline for completion and the client is passive aggressive, unaccountability establishes itself within the very workmanship of the artist. The product, even a solid product, could cause damage if these certain communication issues lead to an unaccountable scenario. Chaos takes over and production potential is undermined.

The best-case scenario in all of this world of unaccountability is the chaos devours itself before an error or mistake is experienced. On an average day, this chaos is routine and makes up the day to day of our organizational processes. On a not so average day, chaos could appear as a far greater threat. If the day ever came in which retribution needs to be taken against the chaos, then the execution must be forceful, tactful, swift and thorough.

The president that showed a lazy front for the entire busy season may get overly comfortable at a board of directors' meetings, leading to an opening for the board to suggest counter action be taken against the initial contract. The employee stamping his or her own time card may not count for certain morning routines as billable, therefore loses out on a set margin over the course of time. The artist who spends four weeks deriving an epic project for a client presentation, only to find out the client is now overwhelmed by the complexity and irrelevance of his or her money spent.

The definitions of chaos in business are limitless, and we in the 21st century are lucky that chaos doesn't show itself as often as a Prince Sado. Rather, most businesses and people attempt to control chaos through ensuring tasks, decisions and initiatives carry with it sessions of accountability on all applicable levels. The dependency on justice in order to eliminate random acts of unproductive chaos in the existence of a business is a cornerstone of mercantilism, the 18th century and the 21st century capitalist theory. Chaos left unchecked will always amount to retribution in some way. Businesses unable to focus energy toward the chaos itself will suffer the acts of retribution directly.

Twenty-seven

Your Greatest Ally

THERE ARE DEFINING moments in any person's life in which the trial of the times establishes the very moment worth defining. It is only when a person is able to succeed over these trials that will allow the outside world the ability to grant any sort of felicitation towards the actions worth recognizing. All other parties simply receive the pleasure of not losing as much as any other poor soul involved in the struggle. France in the mid-15th century was a world of struggle saturated with poor souls attempting to grasp at whatever remaining dignity was left in their demoralized world. The story of France in the mid-15th century is able to be told today simply because there was one soul willing to embrace the faith calling to her from the mouth of her own greatest ally.

In 1412, France was in a fragile peace treaty with England, was being ruled by the mad King Charles VI and was on the verge of being a nation divided by dynastic lineages held by the ruling noble elite. These two factions would come to be known as the Orleanist, or Armagnac, and the rival Burgundians. This civil strife, along with the weak central ruling monarch in Paris, ensured that France was in an enfeebled state ripe for the taking from the opportunistic English under King Henry V.

King Henry V, in August 1415, claimed his family's title to the French throne and set forth conquering most of northern France. One defining battle during this period was the battle of Agincourt when an Armagnac dominated army was utterly annihilated by the invading English. This defeat and the forthcoming invasion was enticement enough for the rival faction Burgundians to pledge allegiance to King Henry V and support his claim to the throne of France.

Charles of Ponthieu, the current French successor to the throne of France, had retreated his court to Bourges in central France. At this time, the trials of France were at their direst form. England and her allegiances surrounded the French loyalists all while the English were beginning to amass an invasion force along the Loire River to finish off the southern French who held out against English occupation. Only the most loyal and least conquered of the French noble class were still aligned with the rightful French line of succession. These steadfast few were experiencing their darkest hour, and it seemed as if only a miracle could save them from eventual English domination.

It is said that Joan of Arc had at a very early age been the witness of visions from God himself, demanding of Joan to practice pious habits and to go to church regularly. Joan was every definition of a simple peasant girl with, at this time, absolutely no hope for advancement in an entirely class-dominated patriarchy. In this era of medieval Europe, a poor girl was perhaps one of the lowest of classes, only good for one licentious thing in the eyes of men. Joan was assuredly different. By the time the English were readying to invade lower France, Joan was receiving visions exclaiming to her the mission on which she was called by God to carry out. It was this mission and the faith in that mission that propelled Joan to proceed on perhaps the most arduous task that any women before her time had ever been tasked to see through.

Joan was given a very specific mission by God to seek out Charles of Ponthieu and to lift the now present siege at Orleans in central France. Orleans was the last strong bastion of French rule under Charles, and its fall would more or less signal the doomed end of the war against the English. Joan had no background in warfare, she had no connections within the noble courts and most importantly, she was a woman seeking audience with a rightful king. Her mission was of the most immense improbability for success that it is hard to imagine very many other occurrences in the history of humanity with less of a chance for success. The insurmountable odds were Joan's area of focus. Her persistence in seeking an audience, her most adept path, and the faith she held within the mission was her greatest ally. After three attempts to seek an audience, she was finally granted just that.

In one of the most iconic encounters in the history of humanity, Joan the peasant girl marched to see the future King Charles amongst his court with nothing more than a vision and no grounds to administer the conclusion she was proclaiming. Charles was completely struck by the faith Joan held within her mission, her task laid forth and their shared belief in God. Before Charles was willing to give a peasant girl his army for use in lifting the siege of Orleans, he sent her to his ecclesiastical advisors to test every inch of spiritual, mental and physical integrity. This illiterate eighteen-year-old girl was subject to immense interrogation of all sorts by groups of well-endowed noblemen—only Joan's undying faith in her mission saw her through these intense levels of interrogation.

Once Joan was proven to be of sufficient caliber according to all of Charles's advisors, she was given an army to march upon Orleans. Men who never in their lives had even vaguely thought of a woman in a man's clothing were now being lead against an overwhelming opponent by a green peasant girl in man's plate mail on horseback. Joan's resolve in the face of these odds could only have been explained by her continued conviction in the message delivered to her by her faith. This conviction was her greatest ally in lifting the hearts of the soldiers around her against the English enemy. There are very few success stories such as this, Joan and her army of Frenchmen had defeated the English laying siege to Orleans.

By the time of Joan's martyrdom at the hands of the English, France had a new crowned king in Charles VI, and the tide of the war against the English had completely turned in the French favor. The English were so afraid of the message delivered by Joan that only by turning her into a martyr was their doom truly realized. The conviction Joan had within her mission was so intense the court upon which she was sentenced to death had known periods of remorse so great that tears were shed in public.

I have always felt as though our 21st century world enjoyed glancing past stories which involved heavy dependence on spiritual faith for the driving factor of the means towards a desired goal. Does faith truly not represent the modern businessman or women in the 21st century? If one turns to the average post on social media or the typical business self-help book, it is hard to imagine a topic more looked over than this one. I would take a bet that the most successful entrepreneurs in history had such an undying conviction towards their mission and vision that one could easily say there was an almost spiritual connection between the person and the goal. If you are pursuing a dream without an intense amount of faith within your product, within your service or within your ability to deliver upon a statement, I would make the argument that your entrepreneurial endeavors may never truly experience the level of success one on average pursues. A true person strong in faith doesn't need a vision or a direct message from a god in order to have belief in one's goal. True faith starts deep within your heart and always seeks to proclaim the unrivalled vision of your entrepreneurial destiny.

Twenty-eight

An Image of Altruism

ONE OF THE SINCEREST habits within 21st century business is the desire to impact the world in a positive way, eventually for the intent to earn a profit. The average businessman or woman tends to view their entrepreneurial endeavors as a means to earn money for self-gain alongside their own organizational success; a humble truth. For many entrepreneurs, the role of the benign profitless citizen falls upon the feet of a not-for-profit organization engaged in the goals of foregoing monetary fruition for the benevolent objective. The wall of difference built by these two distinct organizational structures may seem obvious when thinking about them from an end vs. the means relation. In reality, it is impossible to truly make the claim that an organization, formally to one side of the fence, is actually more or less altruistic than the other.

The Roman Empire at the dawn of the 4th century had its share of successes and challenges to say the least. The empire in terms of land dominance was in an extremely strong position, still holding much of its territory in the west, in the far east and throughout northern Africa. There was no shortage of threats, from both inside and outside the empire, though. The recent reign of Emperor Diocletian saw a major stabilization of the empire in the late 3rd century after a period of much strife. At the end of Diocletian's rule, he materially changed the role of Caesar within the Roman Empire. It was Diocletian who saw that the only way to ensure the Roman Empire retained its vast domain was to divide the territory up into quadrants, each under the rule of an independent Caesar. Diocletian appointed a man by the name of Constantius as Caesar over the Gaul and Britain territories.

Constantius had a son named Constantine, who would come to play a major role within the history of the world.

Now, much of the internal strife within the Roman Empire at this time was due to reasons unnumbered. It was Diocletian's belief that one major component of insurrection within the empire was due to religious changes within the populations across the empire. The pagan religions of old Rome were very quickly falling to the wayside in light of simpler and more modern monotheistic religions from the eastern part of the empire. Diocletian furthered a practice of making a statement against monotheism by persecuting the Christians. The Christians at this time had become the fastest growing minority religious group in the entire empire. Churches had been found all across the empire by the time Diocletian had come into power. The attractiveness of monotheistic religious practice was very present within the majority pagan population. The persecutions were brutal and intense, often made public to ensure a display of gruesome consequence for falling out of the old Roman pagan way.

This tetrarchy was meant to create four territories equal in manageability and in martial power across the empire. When Diocletian died, he left the four new Caesar's in charge of their own distinct region. The hearts of men are filled with hunger for power, paranoia and opportunistic action. Constantine was declared Caesar over all of Rome in 306, immediately after his father's death. This caused an uproar by the other three claimants and a civil war immediately followed. Constantine at first held back against the three other tyrants; his opponents waging war upon one another while Constantine waited in Gaul. Once it had become clear that Constantine could no longer sit idly, he immediately took his legions into the heart of Italy with the intent of taking Rome. Constantine's main opponent in Rome was Maxentius, who lead a far more powerful army than Constantine and currently was entrenched along Constantine's path to Rome.

Their armies met upon the Milvian Bridge over the Tiber River in what some consider one of the most influential battles in the history of the Western World. Constantine prevailed against overwhelming forces, took Rome and became the sole Caesar over all of the Roman Empire. The public opinion at this time was that

Constantine was awarded victory through divine intervention due to his loyalty and faith towards the One Christian God. Soldiers painted the Chi Rho on their shields before the battle and it was also made public that Constantine himself had witnessed a vision proclaiming victory to the faithful. What followed was the end of the persecution of the Christians across the entire empire, the acceptance of Christianity as the primary religion in all of the empire and a biased direction of Rome towards a heavily dominated theocratic Christian infrastructure.

It is an easy thing to solely believe the story of Rome's conversion to Christianity as an act of altruistic, benign and benevolent action. The bloodshed and persecution brought on by the Romans against the early Christians was in its very nature at that time, especially considered by today's standards of social justice—intolerant barbarism against a defenseless minority. Was the action by Constantine solely one with altruistic intent? Were there other personal motivations for having proclaimed all Rome a Christian Empire? Are the baseline facts correct in assuming that all of this change was brought on by one man's desire to end a ruthless purge of his own people? The typical answer to these questions would err on the side of altruism, an act that was a course correction towards the path of tolerance and justice.

When looking deeper into opportunistic reasoning for waging war under the Christian banner and eventually converting all of the empire to a single monotheistic religion, certain crucial conditions arise out of the bright light of divine intervention. The Roman Empire had been in possession of a multitude of eastern regions, up to this point, for many centuries. The eastern way of both religious and political life had over time made a very material impact on the way of life for those in the western empire. Many governments in the east were based solely upon theocratic regimes where emperors allowed themselves to be venerated as divine entities in their positions of power. Anyone entering into court to meet an eastern theocratic emperor was more accustomed to practicing rituals with spiritual context rather than simple bureaucratic designs. It only made sense that the vast population of the Roman Empire sought comfort in a theocratic deity, rather than having the knowledge that any mortal man ruled the macro decisions of daily life. Monotheism made this idea of a divinely inspired single Caesar more in line with the common person's expectations for such roles. The knowledge that one God and one man were in leagues was much easier to conceptualize and internalize compared to having a plethora of pagan gods feuding over which god was more appropriate in any given moment.

Furthermore, the empire had experienced generations of internal civil war throughout the 3rd and 4th centuries. On countless occasions, the rivalries of noble houses had gotten in the way of the health and wellbeing of the empire and her people. Pagan gods and rituals were so various and so varying that traveling to the next village over could have alluded to bouts of strife and conflict across the expanse of the empire. It is hard for the common man and woman to believe their spiritual priorities could differ from that of neighbors both close to home and in faraway lands. It is noted that many early Roman Caesars, Severus and Aurelian, had expressed a desire to appropriate monotheistic religion into their reigns. The unifying principle that a single God could take the place of all pagan gods was an extremely attractive prospect to Constantine, who had inherited an empire he himself had inherited through the use of civil unrest. Many Roman people were easily able to relate a single God to the worship of the sun, the worship of the god Mithra and of course, the one God under Christian and Jewish principle. In this way, Constantine in quick fashion united the largest empire on earth after generations of internal strife through the unification of belief in one Christian God.

There are more times than I can personally count, and I am by my early trade an accountant, in which I have had to listen to a startup pitch that drives home the point of an altruistic ideology. These presenters always try to deliver an image of altruism connected to their product or service that often times is so indirectly correlated that it takes away from the very direction of the presentation altogether. The loss of a solid presentation is, in my opinion, the least concerning moment during a start-ups journeys, but when a naive CEO or founder finds him or herself actually believing in the image of altruism being pitched, this is absolutely the scariest event I witness taking place within a startup world. There are truly very few entrepreneurs motivated by altruistic action, and in many ways this fact is the bedrock in which capitalism is founded.

Now the opposite of altruism is selfish intent, which a lot of times companies fear falling into an image of being the greedy big brother. This is a very real fear for every entrepreneur. Few consumers want to purchase a product from the greedy if their choices allow them the luxury. There is a balance between altruism and greed that needs to be recognized by founders, entrepreneurs, CEOs and anyone in higher leadership. A forced image of altruism when the intent of the business is to make money can lead organizations down paths of no profitability, poor sustainability and high levels of self-destructive ignorance. To know one's place in the scheme of altruistic action, while taking into account the sustainable need to earn compensation for one's product, is the single strongest position to find oneself in order to harness the image of altruism all businesses want to be recognized for.

Twenty-nine

A Time for Profit

IF THERE WERE EVER a man or woman to take an interest in the abundance of wealth available to themselves, without the cautious gaze of onlookers, how would he or she fare when tasked with the ability to understand the consequences of greed? This question has been put to the test on countless occasions throughout history. No better time to study this deeply innate human characteristic of short sighted greed and mismanagement than during the era of kings and queens. This was a time when the decisions of a single man or woman was truly in a world of its own, and the rest of us onlookers were simply trying to follow the intent of that individual, no matter the odds or the futility.

In England, 12th century, it was a time of the high medieval period. Medieval technology had been mastered, to an extent, and the lives of the monarchs had been indoctrinated into every micro and macro way of life for every European nation. King Henry II was a man of intelligence, action and retained knowledge for both languages and law. King Henry had a strong personality, often overcome by his genetically reinforced temperament. Eleanor of Aquitaine had become the wife of King Henry after a divorce with Louis VII, King of France. Eleanor was of an equally strong character and was of the more iconic women of her age. Both King Henry and Queen Eleanor reigned in beautiful, intelligent and powerful fashion.

Henry's reign started in swift motion at restoring the strength of England. Henry was a highly effective administrator, successfully setting about changing both the infrastructure and governance of his domain. Under Henry II, England regained its strength and effectiveness. Henry's reign wasn't without its own strife, for when Eleanor discovered Henry was a serial adulterer, it cast Henry and England into an unprecedented era of scandal. Eleanor painfully took her son, Richard, with her to court in Aquitaine to escape the influence of Henry II.

Eventually, Henry II was determined to see his young son, John, given swathes of land in England while his other three brothers stood rich of title and poor of power. It was this action that turned Henry's three sons against him in a rebellion for England's crown. The young Henry, the rightful heir to the English throne, was determined to see his father overthrown, and the young Henry was supported in this effort by the French monarchy. After a long rebellion, King Henry II retained his throne and initially prevented his sons from unseating their father. The young Henry died after falling ill from what many say was due to his plundering of a wealthy shrine. Eventually the middle son, Richard, was forced to deal with the continued reign of his temperamental father. Richard waged his own rebellion against his father and succeeded where his brothers had failed. Once Richard had obtained a stronger followership than his father, Henry II succumbed to his old age, felt his shame and died. His eldest surviving son Richard I became king of a strong, wealthy and unified England.

Now Richard I, King Richard the Lionheart, had made a promise very early on in his reign to conduct a third crusade for Jerusalem. The third crusade started with immense optimism within Christian Europe. Three of the most powerful rulers of Europe all took up the cross to reconquer the holy land. King Richard, having just inherited a strong and wealthy England, set out obtaining any and all wealth he could muster in pursuit of his crusade. His plundering of England was conducted by all methods available to him. He openly persecuted and robbed the Jews, imposed obscene taxes upon all English classes and sold all manner of offices and lands in England. Richard I went about deconstructing all of the accumulated wealth of his domain in pursuit of his sole focus. There is a saying about Richard that states, "He would sell the city of London, if only he could find a purchaser."

Richard set out on his crusade with the entire wealth of England behind him. Richard lead a strong attempt at taking the holy land, having conquered Acre and feuding with the great Saladin for many years. The third crusade ultimately ended without the capturing of Jerusalem and a truce between King Richard and Saladin. On his way back to England, Richard was shipwrecked off the coast of the Adriatic, was captured by the duke of Austria and imprisoned. The amount of ransom accepted by the duke of Austria for the freedom of Richard was equivalent to two years' worth of annual revenues for all of England. Richard did not spend much time in England, and quickly upon his return an invasion of France was pursued. Richard gained several victories against the French over the course of the long war. It was on one random day, while Richard was out inspecting the siege works, a peasant fired a crossbow bolt and killed the English king.

Richard I's story of pursuing personal goals above all else while being in possession of such a great wealth is only too familiar when discussing that of a 21st century founder in possession of a fruitful business venture. If all goes well for your organization and profitability finally shows its beautiful face after years of persistent effort, there is a right moment for taking out which you knowingly deserve. There are a few key tips that you should be aware of around profitability that typically slip past the average professional's gaze.

Profitability in many contexts does not mean excess cash. It could very well be a non-cash accounting methodology, such as a way to account for inventory, depreciation and other accrual based coincidences. Also, profitability does not represent a loss of future need for that profit, if in fact that profit is in excess cash. Perhaps your business needs a new piece of equipment, pay down some debt or even host an end of year moral boosting party that was promised. Many times, excess money can be used to ensure the next year or so will become more profitable than what was experienced in the current year. Furthermore, profitability does not mean your business finally exists for your sole personal desires. Much like Richard the Lionheart, who had aspired to inherit a wealthy state from his father, viewing profit as a sole means to one's end puts all of the other characters involved in the venture behind the desires of an autocrat. Enough autocratic actions will almost ensure your downfall and most likely the downfall of everyone who looks to you for leadership.

There are not very many examples of selfless action in today's age of social media. Many entrepreneurs get into entrepreneurship because they believe one day it may pay off with the ability to buy an exquisite lifestyle of luxury. There is little doubt that when someone pursues entrepreneurship and for when the day profitability appears, the long-term well-being of everything you worked so hard to acquire must take the forefront of motivation. It is without this selfless logic that many individuals, with even an inkling of success, never truly make it past having just the potential for true wealth.

Thirty

Three Keys of Production

LET'S TAKE A STEP back into an era that is entirely impossible to imagine as having any relevance to today; the ancient era of the Egyptian Pharaoh's. Their rule was both ultimate in dominance and infinite in influence. The ability for one man to dictate the lives of an entire nation without risk of losing significance in the face of followers is a dynamic that has been totally lost to time. The Pharaoh Khufu, who ruled in the 26th century B.C., was a man with absolute control over the destiny of his people. This dominance was a key component in the construction of the only remaining wonder of the ancient world; The Great Pyramid of Giza.

It wasn't enough for Khufu to have dominion over the lives of his people in order to obtain the capability to create one of the greatest feats in human history. At this time, Egypt had amassed an impressive wealth, a sophisticated infrastructure and the population superior to that of any competitor in the ancient world at that time. Centuries of hard fought subjection of the Nile River Valley had ensured a time of stability and peace for the Egyptian Pharaoh. It was this structured gathering of forces that created the opportunity for Pharaoh Khufu to have the capability to construct a tomb for himself, which would give immortality to his name.

So, if we as the outside observer are able to get past the underlying assumption that the capability to construct The Great Pyramid of Giza exists, we can start to break down the key components necessary to undertake this endeavor and ultimately will understand the bridged components belonging to all production initiatives, even to this day. These key components are applicable to the largest and most complex production initiatives of any era while also being completely relevant to any localized productive task in your day-to-day life. While linear order rarely plays with consistency in our lives, in this topic linear order plays a crucial function in regards to the development of the components in interlocking fashion.

The first step Pharaoh Khufu had to let himself embrace was the original inspiration for building a pyramid of such scope. By this century in Egyptian ancient history, tombs had been built for Pharaohs for around four centuries. The stepped shaped tomb of the pyramids had been in practice for some time before this also, therefore the original inspiration for a pyramid wasn't necessarily based in the shape or reasoning for the project. The original inspiration came from the man himself. The vast scale of the project could only truly be imagined by someone with the power to influence the people around him. To walk into a room and explain the desire to build something far greater than anything built previously was only tangible by a man with the belief, as well as being corroborated by everyone else in the same room, that his own life was a divine entity. This inspiration for grandeur came from a firm knowledge that his existence would last forever. To build the greatest tomb of all time is a testament to this embrace of immortality only reminiscent to a man believing in self-divinity.

Now that the Pharaoh had his inspiration for eternal life in both the spiritual and the mortal realms, he needed something intangible in order to further his pursuit at such an extreme undertaking. Ultimately, the process would have fallen short in a linear execution if the motivation to undertake the task wasn't present. It was common practice to have the tomb of a Pharaoh built with the intent to house the treasures, furniture, food and servants the Pharaoh would need in the afterlife. Any simple Pharaoh would have been complacent with a tomb of a scale similar to that of Khufu's ancestors. Pharaoh Khufu desired something far greater for himself and believed in this concept so greatly that it supplied the very motivation for his lifetime achievement itself.

Khufu was motivated by the challenge of the task and the idea that if he truly was a divine power, no attempt was too great without the uniform expectation for an ultimate successful conclusion to that attempt. If the task failed, how could he truly be divine? The second step to any productive task is the establishment and enrichment of the underlying motivations necessary to make progress on any pursued task.

Finally, the key component necessary in order for a successful production of any given task is the tangible execution and application of the idea itself. While no idea is worthwhile to have without the necessary tangible execution to back it up, no physical act is worth its weight without the inspiration for its origin and the backing motivation for its successful conclusion. This step ends all arguments and confirms all theory in the mind of the pursuer.

In order to build the Great Pyramid of Giza, waterways had to be constructed and optimized in order to suit the larger limestone bricks needed for the great structure. Quarries had to prepare the bricks for transportation. Ingenious shaping techniques were used to transform stone into cubes or angles. Mounds were built along the pyramid in order to drag the stones to their desired location. Skilled and obligated labor was required in the tens of thousands including the housing, food and maintenance of these people. Death and dismemberment were common place among the working conditions, as well as the obligated desire to complete the work for their benevolent Pharaoh. The energy undertaken to complete this project in a tangible sense is unlike anything imaginable before antiquity because everything was done by hand, without automation and with a sense of finality. The final key component is action driven by tangible labor. With this labor comes results, and without this labor a dream never leaves the mind of the owner.

While it makes a lot of sense that such an enormous undertaking would require intense levels of tangible labor, the fruitful execution of these efforts is solely grounded in the opportunity for one to have the capability to enact with confidence. If the capability presents itself then the inspiration for the original thought must become realized within the early linear process or else prior methodologies would easily be utilized in order to complete the given task. Once the linear process of true production has been started, the motivation to carry onward with the original idea is the only component necessary in obtaining the persistence needed in seeing an action reach a successful tangible stage. Finally, and without equal, the tangible execution of the task at hand is mandatory in order to ever see through to the fruits of one's endeavors. It is in this entire process that an idea becomes a reality and that production continues to operate as an integral part of your organization's goals.

Thirty-one

The Value of a Minute

THERE ARE MOMENTS in history, beyond foresight, in which the materiality of a single minute of time may become more relevant than one could ever have predicted. When we plan, predict and execute towards a common goal, a component that was once extraneous can easily become a conclusive factor. Time often plays this role within our lives as human traits, such as procrastination and hesitation, but what happens when the value of our immaterial time weighs on our results in an inevitable fashion? No matter how well we did not procrastinate, time still appears to overshadow the objective against all intention.

Our world in 1915 was beset by a war of unimaginable scale. In an early era of mechanical existence, the lives of men and women across the world resembled a primeval existence. Yet, there was no other time in history in which a global war could have appeared so limitless in its reach. The British Empire was at its greatest extent at the onset of The Great War, owning lands and influencing people on every major continent across the globe. The actions of the British high command would directly dictate the fates of people in lands on the exact opposite side of the planet. This was truly an impressive, almost celestial time to be alive, yet the lives of the common person could not have been more human.

As the war among the European powers grinded to an ongoing stalemate, motivation for alternative strategies became an inevitable and constant demand. As first-world global powers fought in trenches across Europe, it was a quick defeat of the Ottoman Empire that the British Empire had decided could signal the turning point in the war against Germany. Russia had been involved in a brutal campaign against the Ottomans since the onset of The Great War, yet similar to that of the western front, no respite was in sight for their efforts. The British predicted if they were to utilize their superior Mediterranean naval capacity, they could launch a ground attack directly into the very heartland of the Ottoman Empire at Constantinople. If the Ottomans were to take the threat seriously enough, then the Russian front would see a downturn in support, and eventually the Ottoman Empire would bow out of the war.

At first, the British took a strictly naval approach at attacking the Ottoman capital region. Heavy bombardment of coastal forts provided a gateway for a ground attack directly into the capital city. These naval attacks, while initially proving unsuccessful, granted enough confidence in the British high command in order to carry out with more aggressive naval actions against more inland targets. As the British Navy began to experience heavy losses, the initiative to pursue a more aggressive infantry sea landing and ground push became more tangible. A force of British, French and newly commissioned ANZAC, Australia and New Zealand Army Corps, were gathered in Egypt to begin the historic campaign.

In a multi-front sea to land invasion, the expeditionary forces intended to quickly take strategic positions along the coast in order to obtain a pertinent ability to further support actions inland. The British were hoping to take the Ottoman's off guard, and while initial land was taken quickly on certain beaches, the Turkish preparation for the invasion ensured that not all landings were successful. In fact, the landing at Y beach, which initially was undefended, turned into a quick defeat after an Ottoman counter attack saw the death of over 700 British soldiers followed by the immediate evacuation of the position. The ANZAC forces were assigned the invasion of Z beach, in which the force landed in disarray and was immediately under fire by Ottoman defensive positions. After a rocky start to the campaign against the Ottomans, the expeditionary forces maintained strategic positions on the peninsula and began the fortification and entrenchment process so well affiliated with The Great War.

At this point in the struggle for land, the British were determined to capture the well defended village of Krithia. At first, straight attacks were used to no avail and resulting in heavy casualties for the British. Eventually, new feint tactics were employed in which artillery would be used to pound an entrenched enemy position. The infantry would soon after feint an attack to expose the surviving infantry units, followed by a continuation of artillery barrages in order to quell the stubborn defenders. Battles to take Krithia resulted in massive losses to the Ottoman side, but the British fared poorly better. Ottoman offenses during the summer season did not have any better results. One particular struggle for the Ottomans was the attack of the ANZAC held beach in which 42,000 Ottomans stormed the well defended ANZAC position, leading to 3,000 dead Ottoman. The ANZAC forces proved their caliber in that battle, and this was the beginning of a culturally defining moment in British opinion of the Australian and New Zealand commonwealth assets.

As Fall was fast approaching, the expeditionary forces were beginning to experience similar signs of attrition from The Great War struggle; substantial cost for nominal gain. A large offensive was planned for August 1915 and would see a collaborative effort between the multinational expeditionary forces in order to attempt to take significant ground from the Turkish forces. One of the earliest phases of the August offensive was to task the ANZAC forces with the acquisition of an extremely vital track of narrow land, called the Nek. The Turkish positions around this land allowed for the domination of the ANZAC efforts below. The joint coordination between the British Navy and the ANZAC 3rd Light Horse Brigade on August 7th, 1915 saw one of the defining moments in World War I play out.

The British Navy was scheduled to bombard the Turkish positions around the Nek followed up by an immediate ceasefire at 4:30 a.m., at which point the 3rd Light Horse was to quickly leave the trenches and assault the Ottoman positions at the Nek. The British bombardment was a poor display of effectiveness and abruptly ended just minutes before the 4:30 a.m. mark. In a display of green uncertainty, poor leadership and lost opportunity, the officers of the 3rd Light Horse decided to wait until the 4:30 a.m. mark to charge the Ottoman defenses. This couple minute delay would cost the ANZAC forces dearly, giving the Ottomans time to re-position their defenses for an effective stance. As the first whistle blew and the first wave left the trenches, the thunderous roar of overwhelming firepower became obvious. The men in the first wave were annihilated. The men from the second wave saw the writing on the wall, yet followed honors protocol, charged out of the entrenchment and suffered the same fate as the first wave. A third and a fourth wave followed to no avail. The sacrifice made that day in light of overwhelming odds still rings in the hearts of the Australian and New Zealand people as a demonstration of honor, pride, faith and courage.

There will always be moments in your life in which you would like to take back a minute or a second hesitation, which had caused loss or missed opportunities. Thankfully, not many of us today have to experience the cost of missed time such as that of the ANZAC forces in Gallipoli. For us today, the lesson in the value of a minute of time is no less important though. Our lives are all just a series of minutes, and decisions made each minute will see us through to death no matter the choice. How we live by those minutes defines how the world views us and how we view the world through our entrepreneurial endeavors. Your business runs on minutes, your time is a currency, just as important as any investor with capital. Prepare for the minutes given to you with the expectation that these minutes might end at any point. Some of the biggest mistakes entrepreneurs make is they perceive procrastination as the only interference in their time management. In reality, the resourceful planning of time, followed by acting without hesitation in pursuit of quality and objective time ensures that we utilize each minute with the most optimum conclusive benefit.

Thirty-two

When Time Runs Out

OH, THESE DREADED WORDS, the befallen moment in the pursuit of a goal when at last you find yourself incapable of asking for more of anything but failure. Many individuals spend a lifetime escaping this dilemma, while others leave a trail of unfinished work throughout their chosen footprints. Often crucial and defining moments in our pursuits potential for success appear only when time has been depleted. Choice in these instances can make it all worthwhile or can lead to the destruction of everything we've worked so hard to obtain.

In antiquity, time held the same value as of today. A New York minute, as they say, was just as fast as a Persian minute some thousands of years ago for our ancestors that walked the earth. Many millennia ago, the Persian empire was vast by all accounts. It spread across the greater Asian continent and reached deep into European and African settlements. Very few discovered peoples were free from the rule of the god emperors of the Persian kingdom. One such divinity was Achashverosh, or Xerxes by our knowledge, who inherited a legendary empire from his father Darius the Great. Xerxes was a man befit to rule people as a god and walk the earth as a man. No treasure was beyond his touch, and no mortal man or woman could say no to his demands. Our story starts when Xerxes decides to scour the vast Persian empire for a queen of such present beauty that her resonance could stun even a god like himself.

Esther had little family left in the world besides her beloved cousin Mordecai, who had spent his life being a father to an orphaned young girl. No understatement could have been more obvious than by exclaiming the beauty Esther possessed. Mordecai knew this of course and spent many days and nights fighting and fleeting the men who came to acquire. Eventually an emperor's henchman came to Mordecai's doorstep and took Esther to Xerxes for a chance to become a queen. In the presence of a blanket group of other beautiful women, Esther won the king's eye and became queen. Unknown to Xerxes, his ruling lords or any of his henchman or women, Esther was of Jewish descent.

The Jewish people in Persia had been forced to migrate after Jerusalem had fallen to the previous Babylonian conquerors, at first slaves and then ultimately given back access to their lands and independence across the Persian kingdom. The Jews were a token presence within the empire, blessed with the gift to keep their God and to keep their lives among the more loyal worshipers of Xerxes. Not all men felt beholden to treat the Jewish people with apathy. There were men in power who wanted nothing but to crush the life out of any foreign people, particularly foreigners who could coexist without punishment.

Haman was one of these men who wished nothing but the destruction of the Jewish people within the Persian empire. At this point, Mordecai and Esther had won much favor with Xerxes and had been bestowed rights of communication with the lords and nobles within Xerxes court. Haman knew that Mordecai was a Jew and that Mordecai spoke with the tongue of his people in Xerxes court of affairs. It was not known that Esther was a Jew, and she was spared the plotting schemes of Haman and his followers. Eventually, Haman was able to cast a light upon the loyalty of his service to Xerxes and obtained power worthy of man sitting beside a god. Haman spent his power wisely in the pursuit of destroying his most hated enemy; the Jewish people.

Haman had discovered a method in which to use a dagger to eliminate the Jewish presence in Persia, all while concealing the action from the eyes of the Jewish observers in the courts. Haman obtained the formal approval from Xerxes to carry out any action he so wished while using the King's voice of authority. This granted Haman unlimited power amongst the people in charge of governing. Haman sent out two decrees using the signature of

Xerxes. One was a decree ordering the governors to arm the population of the empire on the thirteenth day of Adar to carry out violence against an undisclosed people. The second decree was to be opened only on the thirteenth day of Adar and ordered the governors to take violent action against the Jewish people across the empire.

After the plot had been ordered, Mordecai received a vision sent from God revealing Haman's plans to destroy the Jewish people. Mordecai knew that time was limited and that as the thirteenth day of Adar approached, his people were losing the one thing most precious; time. Mordecai took the risk in approaching his orphaned and adopted cousin from a time long past. He met with Esther and informed her of the impending doom, which bewitched her people in all corners of the empire. It was in this moment that Esther had to both choose her loyalties and act with utmost haste due to time running out. Esther had a grand life as queen, and yet her convictions won the day. She chose to side with Mordecai and her people in dismantling the wicked plot of Haman.

There was no possible way to reverse the decree of a god at this time. A god emperor makes no mistakes and pleading with Xerxes to reverse an already enforced decree was impossible. As the grains of sand were falling, Esther had to come up with a plan to protect her people, protect Mordecai, dismantle the powerful Haman and to observe benevolence to her husband. This was no simple feets, yet with the hourglass pouring, there was no time for idle maneuvers.

Esther approached the king and Haman one day in court and in front of all the courts noble lords and rulers, offered to serve dinner to Xerxes and Haman at the next evening. Xerxes was pleased at the invitation and sought nothing but to honor his beautiful queen at the court of his ruling subjects. Haman was only astounded at the offer to dine with the king and queen. The opportunity to dine alone was obviously a sign that his hard work under Xerxes was being rewarded, that eventually the queen herself would come to pay respect to the great Haman.

At dinner the next day, with Haman and Xerxes in attendance and the thirteenth day of Adar fast approaching, Xerxes requested that his queen divulge the reason for the dinner by stating he would give up to half his kingdom for his beloved queen. Esther simply put that her request was to host Xerxes and Haman to a second meal the following evening, and at that meal she would give her request to the king and his right-hand man. On the second evening, Xerxes and Haman shared a meal with Esther. Eventually, Xerxes asked again regarding the reason for the evening's meals, offering up to half his kingdom for his beloved wife. Haman was living in a dream, being offered dinner with the beautiful Esther and the divine Xerxes. The royal nature of these meals and the self-gratifying nature upon which he was chosen hid any thoughts that there was a dual purpose to these meals.

Esther exclaimed to her husband that his beloved queen was of Jewish background, and Haman had plotted against her people to his own personal benefit and gain. She went on to say his decrees saw to the death of her people and went against the very woman a god emperor grew to know, love and cherish. In that moment, Esther took all risk upon herself, at the prospect of losing her own head, when time had all but run out for her people and spoke with selfless action in the defense of every Jew in the Persian kingdom. Xerxes was befit with rage, and Haman was taken by pure and utter horror at the transpiring events.

Haman was both professionally and personally destroyed. His plots overturned by a king's decree that granted all Jewish people in the empire with the right to defend themselves against all aggressors on the thirteenth day of Adar, thus countering the decree sent by Haman without altering his benevolence. Esther won the favor of her husband and saved Mordecai and her people. The Jewish people in Persia became a crucial component in the development of Persia throughout the next couple of millennia and even in the world of today.

The stories of Esther and Mordecai have come to represent a plethora of moral, life and practical lessons, still very relevant many millennia later. It is the perception of Esther's position that we want to focus on here, while she is waiting for that day to come in which her people, that she had become detached from physically, will be annihilated due to the deviance of another. Her ability to sit down and choose a course of action is by far the single most powerful component brought forth through this story for our use as 21st century entrepreneurs. I assure you, and I promise you that your entrepreneurial venture will be faced with a zero-hour moment in which the defining course of your business will be decided in a matter of hours, minutes or even seconds.

The key to finding success in moments like this is to stick to your convictions and weigh heavily the potential to allow outside influence to apply an altercation for your course. Many times, in crucial moments of decision making, allowing an outside force to weigh in on the path can see your business fall in the pocket of a party for which your goals are not the primary focus of their action. Also, these defining moments must be done with the acceptance of risk on your behalf. Every single time a decision is presented, particularly a speedy decision, your job is to analyze the risk of all options. If you are at the fork in the road on a material decision, assuming your own risk can be as easily avoided as if this were a normal decision to make is a fool's thought. As the business owner, as the CEO and as the founder your risk is tied to the life of your business and avoided risk at all costs for your own neck will only ensure that your business suffers from the choices of risk averse action.

Finally, for the purposes of brevity, in moments of hard decisions and multiple parties, the assumption that an option exists for all parties to win only ever slows down the success process for your own endeavors. If your back is to the wall and the clock is ticking, sometimes the only course of action for the health of the business venture is to sacrifice a chicken in order to spare the farm. Not all parties will be able to continue to provide the necessary sustenance for your business as it grows and finds success. Many parties will likely weigh it down and become more of a liability than an asset. In moments of decisiveness, your ability to cut the liable parties and ensure only parties that will contribute to the team carry onward is absolutely crucial.

Thirty-three

The Limits of Effort

OFTEN, WE HEAR THE SIMPLE words spoken, "There is no limit to what you can achieve with hard work and determination." When you are an individual at the early stages of your entrepreneurial journey, these words appear motivating and inspiring. As progress builds, momentum sways your ability to maintain status quo and becomes more of an intricate component than just your ability to grow. Eventually, scale becomes so relevant that it actually becomes a threat to your organization's ability to perform. These realities are hidden from the view of ordinary men and women because the "sky's the limit" idea is far more romantic and motivating to get the workforce out of bed than discussing the realities of scalable limitation.

At the onset of the 1930s, the Russian economy was at the beginning of a major industrial reshaping. The Russian world was one of backbreaking agrarian rule, and the majority of the workforce was destined to farm the vast Russian landscape to feed the recently transformed communist population. This workforce provided services beyond just farming though. Shoemakers had to make shoes for the agrarian population, blacksmiths had to make tools for the agrarian population, carpenters built houses, mothers took care of the future agrarian workforce and merchants traded goods of plenty for goods of scarcity. An entire national economy was built upon the toiling of the soil; it was an economic staple that had seen the Russian people through a millennium of macro and micro trials.

Russia had relatively recently become a communist nation at the onset of World War II, a mere two decades earlier. The system of government was still in a trial by error development stage, with the ambitious Joseph Stalin determined to see Russia as a leader in the modern mechanical world. Stalin set forth transforming Russia into an industrial giant in order to keep up with the western powers. Years of infrastructure redesign and redirection during the early 1930s saw the initial shift toward a large portion of the population being moved into manufacturing and industrial jobs. The population began to shift from a purely agrarian world to a more modern mix of dense urban industry surrounded by scattered rural farmsteads.

By 1937, Russia was on par with the western powers in terms of industrial productive power. Eventually, history caught up with Stalin as Hitler's Third Reich broke the alliance between Russia and Germany. The German mechanized war machine was traversing directly for Leningrad and Moscow.

The Germans were fast, heavily armored, well supplied, proficiently skilled and supremely determined to destroy Moscow as fast as humanly possible. At the backs of resilient half-tracks, the panzer grenadier legions were followed by companies of hard hitting panzer tanks during the Operation Barbarossa. The initial conquering of Western Russia by the Germans was lightning fast. Within no time at all, the Russian professional army was in shambles, and Adolf Hitler was only a few battles away from having officially seized Moscow; an accomplishment no mortal man has laid claim to.

Stalin and the Russian people were at a crucial moment within their nation's survival. On the verge of defeat against an overwhelming enemy, Stalin used a ruthless tactic of further transforming the Russian economy into a pure military industrial powerhouse. One of the most remarkable accomplishments of the entire global theatre of war was the redistribution of the industrial arm from western Russia to eastern Russia, leading a mass migration of people of the which was never seen before in such a short period of time. In early 1941, the Russian industrial and resource capabilities were given over entirely to the military regime. By the end of 1941, the production output of the Russian military industry was two to three times higher in almost all major military categories of produced equipment and supplies. The growth in production of armaments, supplies, tanks and weapons was astonishing.

As the war with Germany started to grind into a war of attrition, in which both sides were fighting in battles with little gain and almost no end in sight, the Russian need to keep up with industrial production continued to grow. The idea that the nation with the most produced materials of war would eventually outperform the other was the basic strategy of this time. Russia needed more guns, tanks, bullets, shells and soldiers. The allotment of resources to the military industry in Russia by 1942 had increased by some factors as high as three to four times the levels in 1941. As much as 68 percent to 75 percent of certain resources, such as fuel and high-grade steel, were being consumed by the military industry, while many in the consumer economy had to forgo access to these raw materials entirely.

As the usage of resources by the military industry continued to grow, and the economy as a whole began to shrink. By the end of 1942, the economy of Russia had contracted by around 40 percent. For every liter of fuel given to the military industry, the output from that fuel had diminished by an exceedingly increased rate into 1943. As more steel was given to the military industry, every other consumer driven industry would deteriorate, leading to the cost of steel overall to increase. Eventually, the ability for Russia to produce a tank became exceedingly more expensive than the previous tank built by the same factory. Russia as a military industrial powerhouse had reached its limit of production potential. Only by taking more resources and more people away from civilian jobs and consumer industries would Russia start to dismantle the economy for which gave Russia the ability to become a powerhouse in the first place.

It wasn't until 1943 that the problems with diseconomies of scale of the Russian productive output of the military industry started to cease. Russia eventually won the Battle of Stalingrad through military sacrifice and German exhaustion. Once this central front opened up, the Russian style of overwhelming massed attack began to weigh heavily on the already stretched thin German front. This, combined with resource assistance from the allied nations and direct expansion in resource allocation to civilian production saw the relief from the overly burdened military industry. The war was won as the Russian military industrial diseconomies of scale began to take shape. If the war had carried on any longer than it had, Russia may have lost the war of attrition due to an economic collapse from within.

There are almost no differences at all between the capabilities of thriving healthy business in the 21st century compared to that of the diseconomies of scale experienced by Russia during World War II. Perhaps the only difference is that Russia was fighting a war of attrition against an aggressive fascist regime, but when discussing the scope of scalability, the difference is negligible. All large organizations and corporations on this planet experience the same problem of scalability that Russia had experienced in World War II. Solutions to problems that include investing significant resources into other departments only strip the resources from supporting departments. Hiring employees here will always limit the hiring of employees there. Focusing solely on customer service can take away from the quality of product you offer and over time will lead customers to not care at all that your customer service is exceptional if their product falls apart at the seams. Only by realizing that diseconomies of scale can happen at a tangible and intangible level, at every frontend and backend of the business, will you be able to strike the right balance for continued production and success.

Thirty-four

The Reliance on Opposites

BEFORE THE ATTACK ON Pearl Harbor, The United States of America was viewed as an underdog by some and a sleeping giant by many. All major nations engaged in the World War II conflict had seen mass migration of portions of their population over to the United States since the end of The Great War. It was apparent that this nation, untouched by war, would eventually play a major role in the outcome of the war. While the industrial arm of the United States was on the minds of all the foreign powers involved in the war, it was the military leadership that was the undercurrent ripping through the fabric of global military might. Of the hundreds of generals that had taken up arms during the war globally, the competent, spirited and always publicized generals of the United States proved that the new-world power had the diversity in leadership necessary for ushering in the post-war age.

Out of all the generals to choose from during the war effort by the United States, there is no better example to demonstrate the diversity of leadership than by examining the three generals Marshal, Eisenhower and Patton. These three leaders all had exceptional military careers and by many accounts are three of the greatest examples of what it means to be a leader in not only the U.S. military, but also in the history of warfare of all time. For the purposes of our analysis, we are going to acknowledge early on that each of these men had illustrious careers, served in both world wars, were educated by the best military academies, were restricted to the same rules of conduct in accord with the U.S. military and all three were involved within the same military initiatives during the invasion of Europe and North Africa

The campaigns that we are going to discuss are only two of the major campaigns from the allied invasion of Europe in the west. The two campaigns selected were optimum for this story due to the relevant nature each man played in their ultimate victory. The first campaign will be the allied invasion of North Africa, Sicily and Italy at the onset of the war. The second campaign will be the U.S. Army's march toward Western Germany. These two campaigns were the stuff of legends, and the three generals we are discussing in this chapter all had a various hand in seeing the mission through to a masterful success.

General Patton was by all accounts a man of tenacity, an inspirational leader of men on the front lines and a pragmatic personality that often clashed with the changing doctrine of politicized war of the modern era. Patton was viewed as a soldier more akin to fighting in the wars of antiquity than in the modern wars of the politician general. During the North African campaign, Patton exceeded expectations and delivered the green troops of the U.S. to victory against the battle-hardened vets under Rommel, the Desert Fox. In the European campaign, Patton was the top field general overseeing the day-to-day initiatives of the U.S. Third Army as it conquered its way through France and Germany.

Patton was a master tactician focused on hard hitting speed and the relentless gaining of ground so the enemy could never have enough time to prepare. He had pioneered armored company tactics before and during the war, leading the lighter armored Sherman tanks to countless victories against the thick armor and stronger guns of the German panzer and panther divisions. The tactical aptitude of Patton demonstrated his ability to understand the minutia of battle with speed and reliability in decision making. One of the best quotes from Patton regarding our studies here was, "Tactics is the daily lot of all. Splendid strategy may be made abortive by poor tactics, while good tactics may retrieve the most blundering strategy."

General Eisenhower, a man of tactful character, was the ideal kind of man it took to influence the strong personalities of Patton, Bradley and Montgomery. Eisenhower commanded the respect from the field officers on the front lines while maintaining the strictest adherence to his leadership from all staff officers in the

European theatre. Ike, as the propaganda machine loved to reference him by, was a grand strategic mind in the overall allied theatre of war in Europe and North Africa. From D-day to V-day, no macro strategic option wasn't sent up to Eisenhower for a stamp of approval. The day to day opportunistic tactical positions during the war were made possible because of the strategic initiatives of Ike and his staff. During the North African campaign, Eisenhower was crucial to ensure lines of communication stayed open between the multiple branches of military might commissioned to the Mediterranean.

While tactical presence on the field of battle was left to field officers, Eisenhower was the liaison between the foot soldier on the front lines to the politician generals in D.C. Logistical problems were a common concern for Eisenhower during the war. Ensuring the troops were supplied with the necessary equipment to be effective on every single day of the war was of the utmost importance. This grand scale strategic awareness fell on Eisenhower's shoulders and everyone looked to this man for a strong centralized approach at conducting the war from a board room. While Patton was deciding upon which tank formation to use to conquer an enemy position, Eisenhower was ensuring that the tanks were manned, fueled, supplied and positioned for effective execution of their most savage role.

General George Marshal in this era of American history was a name heard on the radios in every household across the country for decades. He was the person people associated with as looking out over the interest of the United States from a political perspective before, during and long after the war. Marshal was a great staff officer with a history of logistical, personnel and administrative management beyond that of normal experienced staff officers. His role during World War II was Chief of Staff, reporting directly to President Roosevelt on all matters pertaining to military relevance. Marshal oversaw ensuring there was a smooth-running command at the highest American levels. He held the president's trust beyond doubt, being consulted in most decisions regarding the conduct of the war. Being this close to the Commander and Chief meant Marshal had to be strategically aware of the military situation, politically present at the highest of levels and was responsible for selling the president on every major initiative push that came across his desk from men like Eisenhower and MacArthur.

Marshal was instrumental in the North African campaign by using his diplomatic skills to alleviate concerns the British commanders had when interchanging with their American counterparts. It was with Marshals help that the decision was made to bomb the Germans around the clock, leading to the catastrophic infrastructure losses suffered by Hitler's forces during the war. Marshal worked directly with Eisenhower in inspecting beachheads for the Normandy invasion and was a key reason why FDR gave his stamp of approval on the risky endeavor. One of the main reasons why Patton was given a high-ranking field position as head of the 3rd Army was due to the overwhelming confidence Marshal had in Patton's field abilities. After the war was over and Europe was suffering from insurmountable losses, it was Marshal who headed the plan to rebuild Europe. The Marshal Plan, as it was called, was pitched to congress and funded by the U.S. government giving Western Europe the edge it needed in seeking post war tranquility against the rising threats from communism in the east. Marshal was the voice of every man and woman who served in the military to the ears of the politicians in Washington.

Patton was a proven battlefield commander, master tactician and often seen present with the common foot soldier along the front. His leadership at the micro level ensured the U.S. was up to the task of winning the war against Germany in the hard-fought battles, which saw the sacrifice of countless soldiers during the war. Eisenhower oversaw the grand stratagem, communicating with multiple parties to ensure communication was never broken among the allied parties. He governed one of the greatest logistical undertakings in the history of mankind, feeding and fueling the American troopers on their march to Berlin. Marshal was present for all grand strategy sessions during the war but was most prevalently present alongside the army of politicians who had the U.S. military under a microscope throughout the duration of the war. His efforts in solving global problems as a military general ushered in a new era of generalship that can still be witnessed today with the modern generals in the U.S. military. Marshal was also awarded a Nobel Peace Prize for his work in saving Europe from utter devastation and saving the world from fascist rule.

While it may seem like a major undertaking to compare the World War II global theatre to any small, medium or even large capitalist organization of the 21st century, the principles are very much the same. The need for a diverse group of leaders to oversee the intricacies of any organization is mandatory for success. Whether that is a COO with gift for tactical analysis along the product side, a CEO with the ability to politic with the best of them and yet get down to basics with the design team, or a CMO whose sole job is to sell a product or service to a world of skeptical consumers. A business needs the diverse skillset, and no one personality can see an entire organization through every task or challenge that may present itself along the course. Your best foot forward would be to embrace the differing viewpoints, colorful characters and wildly vast personalities needed to see your business become the well-oiled machine it was always meant to be.

Thirty-five

A Small Window

THERE COMES A TIME in any prolonged endeavor in which a party subject to an opportunity is presented with the choice to act. This choice to act can present itself for either a short or long duration of time, depending on the situation. Almost all examples of legendary achievement come from choosing the optimum time to act without hesitation. Weeks, months and years worth of waiting and preparation can lead to a window of opportunity so small, to miss it may seem like any ordinary day.

Continuing our World War II narrative, in 1940 the European, Asian and African continents were all engaged in raging warfare. In the west, the Japanese had created a Pacific Rim empire that had seen the domination of China, Southeast-Asia and most of the Pacific Island nations. In the east, the Germans were marching on Russia, France, North Africa and Egypt. The United States at this time was currently fighting an internal debate on whether involving itself in another global European and Asian conflict was worth the investment. The isolationist perspective was prevalent in America due to the recent Great Depression and World War I conclusion. With such divisive positions at every dinner table across the nation, it is hard to imagine America could have been in a place to notice such a fragile window of opportunity for which it came to partake.

The years following up to the Japanese bombing of Pearl Harbor were a cautious approach at choosing sides and positions for the global war. The first peacetime draft was issued, warships were given to England, Naval strengthening of U.S. assets in the Pacific and embargoes of goods to Japan and Germany had very easily concluded upon what side the U.S. was fighting on. Many of these political decisions were unpopular at home due to isolationist opinion. Once the Japanese bombed Pearl Harbor in December 1941, it was clear the U.S. couldn't act as an isolated nation any longer. The war came to the homestead, and mass support for the war effort and the military indoctrination of American life became a welcoming sight. But it wasn't until Pearl Harbor, in December 1941, that America had declared war upon Japan and Germany. Also, it wasn't until November 1942 did the invasion of North Africa take place, and D-day didn't occur until June 1944. While it appears reasonable the U.S. would declare war after directly being attacked, the writing was on the wall in August 1939 when Germany had invaded Poland. Why did the U.S. wait until June 1944 to start the final march on Berlin? What would have happened if this choice to act had been shifted to a different window of time?

So, let's play the hypothetical game in this chapter to guess what may or may not have happened if the U.S. had declared war before December 8th, 1941. For logic's sake, let's use the day that France and England declared war on Germany, September 1939. The U.S. could have removed all doubt from the world's minds as to their eventual motivations if they had followed their allies into war on day one. At this time, France was still independent, and Russia was in an alliance with Germany. If Hitler had known the U.S. was going to be aggressively involved in defending against Nazi offensives, the choice to betray Russia may never have happened until England was taken. France would most likely still have been destroyed due to the speed at which it occurred after France had declared war; less than one year. Hitler may have focused his attention on the western front before ever setting foot in Russian territory. If the U.S. would have been stuck in a protracted war with Germany and Japan without Russian involvement, it is hard to imagine that the U.S. would have come out on top.

In our alternative example, we are going to use the hypothetical scenario where the United States would have waited even longer to invade Western Europe. The D-day invasions were so risky and so dangerous that their cancellation entirely was on the minds of several high-ranking officials during the years it took to plan such an endeavor. Perhaps the U.S. would have been more inclined to finish the war with Japan first, defend England and attempt to conquer Germany through the Bavarian region after the conquering of Italy. In either case, if the U.S. would have delayed a western invasion by even a month, the catastrophic event that would have taken place to Germany and many nations in Western Europe would have been devastating. When the Red Army was approaching Eastern Germany in 1944 and 1945, their tenacity was ruthless. The amount of rape, murder and devastation reaped upon the German people by the Red Army in the east cannot be debated. If the U.S. and British Allies were even one month behind their actual schedule, the Russians would have taken Denmark, all of Berlin, and possibly Belgium and Western Germany along the Rein River. The following Cold War period would have been vastly different, with the Russians having a deeper hand in western affairs, going so far as removing the German presence completely from the face of the earth. By the U.S. entering the war exactly when it did, it spun a timeline of events that protected the western world, democracy, capitalism and the 21st century as we know it today.

World War II was such a complex war with so many parties involved that the hypothetical scenarios could be played through the minds of experts for generations of academic study. The resulting power struggle between the U.S. and Russia would have been changed completely had the U.S. not attempted to enter the war exactly when they did. Hindsight is the king of historical sciences, and it is hard to imagine a world so different than to think of what the United States and the world could have become had FDR not acted as quickly as he did within one day of the Japanese attacks on Pearl Harbor.

Your entrepreneurial endeavors fall into windows of opportunistic decision making. For most businesses, well-orchestrated planning phases can lead to periods of long dead time, awaiting that fateful day when a client opportunity comes knocking at the door. Perhaps your organization is waiting for the right time to launch open beta, go live or go to market. There are many promising business models that enter the market too early and scare away customers with potential due to unproven offerings. When a client does finally call, perhaps moving too cautiously in not wanting to make a mistake can throw a customer off. Making them feel as though your confidence in the product leaves much to be desired. Always prepare the classic elevator pitch, a speech in under 20 seconds, that can give a high-profile individual a glimpse into your venture with enough time to keep that person's interest long after they have written you off. Preparation and execution is worthless without opportunity, and opportunity ceases to exist without the competence in labeling exactly the right time to pull the trigger and move forward.

Thirty-six

A Motivating Voice

IN ANY GREAT TALE there are a few character types worth mentioning, and one of these is always the protagonist. The protagonist is typically the one we are betting our hopes on seeing come through as victorious in the end and usually always the character with the most cards stacked against themselves. There are many different personality traits of a protagonist; including moral principle, undying resolve and, the crowd favorite, lifelong underdog. There is one trait that certain characters may possess, can even be held by the dreaded antagonist at the tale, that truly sets them apart from the other characters involved in the plot progression. This one skill is an ability to use words as a weapon for inspiration, motivation and actionable influence all leading to positive anticipation by the remaining characters.

The protagonist in our tale here has been romanticized to an almost legendary place in history, even in modern times. William Wallace was a commoner in Scotland during the 13th and 14th centuries. There is not a lot of hard evidence to support a detailed account of William Wallace, most likely due to his humble origins and the trials for which Scotland was facing at the time. What is known is that Wallace was at the highest level; a middle-class man in the Kingdom of Scotland. Before Wallace ever enters our story, Scotland was plagued by poor leadership from its rightful monarch, King John Balliol. Now King Balliol was not a strong ruler and saw to the collapse of Scottish independence. In 1296, he was able to unify an army of resistance against a foreign oppressor, King Edward I, who had gathered himself a large army and set about conquering Scotland under the English domain. This initial invasion of Scotland was ruthless, saw to the annihilation of towns and its people without restraint. When King John and his army had met King Edward on the field of battle, the overwhelming defeat of the Scottish army ensured that England would remain in control of the Scottish lands for many generations to come.

At this time, Scotland was ruled by an oppressive ruler, with no anointed king and a quelled population of commoners without the means to fight or defend themselves in an efficient manner. The nobles, with the unifying power in Scotland, were busy fighting for the petty favors of the ruling King Edward. The rightful King of Scotland, Robert Bruce, had to remain subservient to King Edward or risk continued degradation of his lands and people. The common person was subject to all sorts of brutal English rules and regulations, having no means to gather enough resistance to make a stand against well armored cavalry formations and English ruthlessness.

This is when William Wallace, a common man without title to the rights afforded his noble overlords, decided to make a name for himself and his people. With the overwhelming repression sought by the English, Wallace gathered enough might and influence to plunder the local English sheriff, freeing his small region from English governance in the short term. Wallace knew the English would be back to seek revenge upon his band of upstarts. It is at this point that Wallace became more than just a rebellious peasant and succeeded in liberating several towns across the Scottish Lowlands. As Wallace continued to unify the common population under his voice and banner, the nobles in Scotland began to take notice. Many noble lords were busy attempting to consolidate their privileges with King Edward by disassociating themselves with the upstart rebels. King Edward was hopeful that the rightful leaders of Scotland would be enough to quell any tension that the commoner class could pose; he could not have been more wrong.

It was at this point that the English had decided to make an example of the rebellious Scots by sending a large army of men to the north, including a large contingent of heavy cavalry. Wallace brought to the fight an army of commoners with very little to no formal martial training and without superiority in numbers. The scrappy band of peasants were up against the English professional army supported by a large contingent of heavily armored cavalry, an absolutely deadly force during warfare at this time. Wallace knew that the mandatory step to invading Scotland was by crossing the Stirling Bridge over the Forth river. The English were so overly confident facing a force of poor farmers, they began to cross the bridge using the cavalry as its Vanguard. As soon as a large portion of the cavalry was over the bridge, Wallace and his men descended upon the English. A select group of Scotsmen had set off to hack away at the bridge supports, seeing to the collapse of the bridge and the drowning of several armored men and horse. With the English army unable to support the men across the river, the cavalry were utterly butchered. The remaining army retreated to England, subject to ambush and slaughter by the Scots who were ready to spring the final trap during the fall back. With one well-orchestrated battle, Scotland was relatively free from English rule.

Having been claimed the savior of Scotland by the common men and women, the noble lords of Scotland began to pay respect to the lowborn hero. Robert Bruce went about claiming Wallace a Guardian of Scotland, lifting his rank and title to something of power and nobility. With camaraderie, spirit and diligence did Wallace lead the people to acts of greatness. With power, influence and action did Wallace earn a place among the noble lords.

Wallace's story did not end here. His newly earned nobility was a threat to many of the more cowardly lords in Scotland, who many were still determined to seek favor with the English crown. When King Edward had sent his own personal army up to Scotland to reconquer the lands, it was Wallace and the Scottish nobility that stood to face him. While Wallace and his countrymen were prepared to fight heavy cavalry in melee, King Edward used his longbowmen to outperform the Scottish. The final cutting blow to Wallace was the betrayal of the noble lords who had brought the Scottish cavalry to the battle, for they retreated from the battle leaving Wallace and his army to defeat. While Wallace lived to continue his fight for Scottish independence, it was the rightful King Robert Bruce who took over the momentum started by

Wallace and turned it into a final battle that turned back the English once and for all.

It is easy to look at the story of William Wallace and say, "But wait, Wallace was defeated and betrayed by the noblemen. What kind of leader ends up losing the fight?" You see, if we were to look at every story in history with the expectation that the protagonist gets to finish every fight and see to the final death blow of every villain, we would be missing the most important aspects of what it takes to be a hero in the first place. The final nail on the coffin is not the story of a man or woman's life. William Wallace was the instigator that awoke the drive for an already beaten nation to achieve great feats of defiance. William Wallace, through inspiration and a common plea, took a people without power and gave them more power than even the noblest of lords. With power and influence do people of stature garner the motivation to look upon you as an equal. Wallace's story demonstrates that even during a time of strict class systems and immense wealth disparagement, men and women will always have the power of the spoken word to overcome great obstacles of malfeasance.

Thirty-seven

The Power of the Collective

BY THE MIDDLE AGES, the western and eastern worlds had built and created civilization more parallel with the modern world than of the barbaric world of our ancestors from antiquity. The rule of law sanctioned by complex government institutions ensured day-to-day life was conducted with little to get in the way of filling a lord's coffer. Peasant life was focused on broad work initiatives. Everything from food production to art and services was the focus of an ever diversifying and specializing workforce. Walls, professional armies and logistical infrastructure ensured that civilization maintained the ability to avoid any backward progress. It was a time where the progression of humanity was noticeably distinguishable from that of our ancestors from the more barbaric times. One man had the ability to put this all to the test with the singular power of a collected people.

In Mongolia during the middle ages, there was a culture more reminiscent of a time far earlier than what even the ancient Romans or Chinese claimed to have tamed. The nomadic Mongolian tribes lived by the rules of the hunter and gatherer, staking claim to which they could take for themselves. The largest tribe usually always won over a smaller band. Luck and survival were synonymous to all men, women and children. It was a demonstration into what humanity had evolved from.

One day, a baby was born clutching a blood clot into a small tribe. This young Mongolian boy experienced adversity not uncommon to that of many children in his world of existence. His father was murdered by a rival tribe, he had killed his own brother because of a selfish act after a successful hunt and his tribe was raided and conquered. By the time Temujin was a man, his loyalties had shifted several times across a spectrum of tribes and families. The one constant was his loyal friend and his position as head over his family. As his family had gone through the day-to-day cruelty that was the Mongolian lifestyle, there came a point when Temujin took his first steps at creating a unified Mongolia.

His first action was in pledging service and loyalty to a large tribe whose own khan held close bonds with Temujin's father. This action saw Temujin rise quickly as a leader within this faction due to his superior people skills, wise decision making and enhanced leadership. Most importantly though, was Temujin's ability to revoke the old ways of Mongolian tradition to make room for a more meritocratic system of rule. This reinvention of the Mongolian hierarchal structure meant that lower classes of people had an ability to raise in power based upon significant action. Armed with the power of a new army, Temujin set about a path of revenge that would further stabilize his family's position in a place of leadership. As things were progressing, a major setback occurred when Jamukha, Temujin's most loyal friend, declared an open rebellion against Temujin due to the revolutionary methods in which a meritocracy operated. This rift saw the collapse of Temujin's power within this tribe, and he then set out away from the Mongol tribes to earn fame among others.

By setting himself apart as a strong leader over the course of the next decade, Temujin had regained much of his power under the Jin culture. The Jin were a rival confederation to the Mongols, and this is where Temujin set his family's roots of influence. Under the Jin umbrella, Temujin set out conquering tribes of people using methods never before adapted by any tribe in this warring region. By awarding people on an accord of merit over birth right, Temujin created an upper-class worthy of the titles bestowed upon them. Any conquered tribe was not butchered, scattered and enslaved but rather protected and integrated into the host. These maneuvers away from traditional custom saw Temujin and his tribe grow in power and at a speed unseen before.

As Temujin grew in power, new and old rivals alike fought against the changing storm being ushered in. A key ally, Toghrul was one of the first khans to rebel against the growing power of Temujin. Toghrul's alliance with Jamukha was a dire threat to Temujin and his people. This struggle would prove to be confirmation of everything Temujin was destined to become. Using superior tactics never before seen in the region, Temujin organized his army into squads of cavalry utilizing methods of communication such as flags for tactical efficiency. Armed with bow, dagger, spear and shield, the superior tactics of Temujin conquered and defeated his rivals Toghrul and Jamukha.

Once the major internal rivals of Temujin were destroyed, he began his consolidation over the remaining confederations in the region. These later battles demonstrated a desire for intelligence gathering and the establishment of spy networks over opponent's factions. Armed with knowledge over an enemy, who were a unified and motivated people, superior consolidated powers and efficient tactical procedures, Temujin went on to conquer all of the remaining rival factions. These united people under Temujin were renamed the Mongol Empire, and Temujin was renamed Genghis Khan, ruler of all the Mongols. For the first time in history, the nomadic singular tribes of a multitude of rival confederations were joined under one banner.

The speed at which Genghis Khan conducted war was brutally efficient. With the love for his people, he marched south and east and set about conquering the Xia dynasty and the Jin dynasty. This forced vassalage upon what is now known as modern China. Genghis Khan then went south and west to subject the people of Qara Khitai, which saw the Mongol empire reach as far east as the Muslim nations near the Lake Balkhash. At this point, Genghis Khan saw to the health and infrastructure of his new empire. Establishing techniques such as writing, advanced medicine and centralized commerce, Genghis Khan saw to the long-term establishment of a civilization for his people. One of the most important demonstrations of this initiative was the pursuit of trading partners with the Persian Muslim empire, called the Khwarazmian dynasty, in the South along the Silk Road.

By sending a caravan to establish trade authority with neighboring empires, Genghis Khan was intent on a civilized approach at generating continued wealth and power. The caravan was not well received and was destroyed without hesitation by a local governor. Genghis Khan was determined to establish peaceful ties to the Persian Emperor and went about sending three ambassadors to the Shah. The Shah killed all three men and sent back the head of one of the ambassadors to Genghis Khan as an answer to his request. Genghis Khan set about with 100,000 men in conquering the Khwarazmian dynasty and reached as far east as to the border of modern day Russia and Georgia. After Genghis Khan's death, his sons and grandsons continued to expand the empire as far reaching as modern-day Hungary, Turkey and Vietnam.

The empire under Genghis Khan was, at this point, the single largest empire in all of history and still retains this title today. Through the power of revolutionary thinking, followed by persistent action and expedient unification, Genghis Khan was able to take a nomadic people and turn them into the largest empire the world has ever seen. The power of the collective has never been more effectively demonstrated than by Genghis Khan and the Mongolian people. Genghis Khan held a love for his people above all other things, and through sheer determination, brutality and cunning was he able to usher in the modern world to a culture 3,000 years behind in development.

As Genghis Khan once said, "One arrow alone can be easily broken but many arrows are indestructible." The entrepreneurial world of the 21st century follows this same exact set of rules that Genghis Khan used to become a legend. A unified team of people is beyond doubt a stronger force to be moved. A company that grows through unity is able to conquer a market far greater than that of a disunited force. Revolutionary thinking and strategies followed by persistent action can inspire stragglers to join forces. A culture of unification and consolidation is by far superior to that of repression and dominance. To view employees as conquered subjects will only go so far as to their potential, but to consolidate their own individual cultures into your collective culture will strengthen both the organization and the individual. There is truly no limit to what a company can become by keeping revolutionary progress as a core element of company plans. Perhaps the idea that any single employee is no greater than the company as a whole is the cause of many organizations to plateau. While we understand that unification is superior to disunity, perhaps the empowerment of the individual within that unification is what can create a collective worthy of legendary achievement. If we keep our individuality as we pledge homage to a group, perhaps it is both the group and the individual that gains rather than just one or the other.

Thirty-eight

The Human Element

IT IS RARE FOR a problem within human existence to continue without the growing desire to solve or alleviate the underlying issue. This innate human quality has been at the core of almost every major technological advancement as far back as we can trace. While the application of this human quality has varied greatly over the millennia, the formula for staying power behind technological advancement has stayed identical to its initial approach; advancement that solves a problem is pursued as the new norm. Beyond what becomes the new normalcy within our ever-advancing world, the dependency over these norms begins to tear away at the fabric of what the early problems actually were.

During the First World War, electricity was still a new technological advancement. In fact, most homes in the west still did not have access to electricity by the onset of the war. Urban environments were quickly being developed to have electric street lamps, homes with telephones and the common ownership of radios. The rural areas of most western nations rarely had access to the power of electricity. One could easily say that the dawn of electricity was in many ways similar to that of consumer access to the internet in the early 21st century. As the consumer was given access to electric powered lighting for their homes, the archaic problems of candlelit homes began to subside into mere nostalgia.

When the war broke out, the need for electricity throughout the western front became a major focus for all western generals. Troop movement, vehicles, armament, industry and communications were being revolutionized at breakneck speed to give their own side an advantage over the opponent. Nowhere was this technological development seen so openly than in the utilization of the telephone by the military arms of each nation. As the war changed from that of cavalry and skirmish to stationary trench line warfare, the need for consistent communication across the western front became more and more material. As the spider web of trenches spun from northern Belgium to Southern France, the colossal infrastructure needed to provide communication to all troops began to unfold as an equally colossal undertaking. Throughout the course of the war, hundreds of miles of cable telephone wire were run across the entire western front.

This cable was important in more ways than can be listed within this text. Everything from troop movement, artillery requests, enemy spotting, timing of attack and defense, redeployments, logistical concerns, resupply, cohesion and joint command all were substantially impaired if the cable telephone system was compromised. Entire companies of men oversaw the laying of telephone lines deep underground so that the mass of trenches could reach a listening ear. Artillery bombardment was a great threat due to the scope of usage during the course of the war, therefore the deeper lines could be placed into the earth, the better. As trenches traded hands numerous times throughout the war between sides, the ability of the enemy to intercept communication across open channels became an apparent risk throughout the war. These cable lines were simple compared to our modern infrastructure, one end with a phone and another end with a switchboard to monitor traffic. Multiple calls coming through on a network of lines was common, and the management of these electrical signals was placed into the hands of trained men and women.

Fighting in a trench for months on end during this war was an experience that hopefully no one should experience again, for the conditions were hellish. If a telephone line was destroyed on the front-line trench, volunteers would have to be requisitioned in order to run a message or a manual line for continued communication to remain unhindered. Without the constant reporting of front line trenches to higher commands, the entire trench framework on that side became fragile to enemy exploitation. Artillery bombardments must be reported when occurring so that counter strategies could be implemented. Enemy reinforcements must be reported so that the necessary reserves could be ushered in to stop a pending offensive. Medical emergencies and food shortages were only ever addressed when a line of need could be sent to centralized command. Without the availability for lines of communication to be constantly open, the hellish conditions of trench warfare would have carried into oblivion.

While the dependence on cable communications became an ever-growing phenomenon throughout the war, one article always remained consistent; the human voice on the other end of the line. It didn't matter what element of usage the cable telephone was being used for, the end result always came about by an application through human hands. Soldiers on the front, commanders in the back and logistics in the middle were uniformly a human consistency. Just think that thousands of souls lost their lives just to ensure that the electric telephone continued to operate as a standard along the front. The dependence on this advancement became analogous to an addiction worth spending the lives of men and women to maintain. Human presence at both ends of that telephone always remained true, for the initial problem wasn't the absence of human presence in that front trench but rather the method in which that human presence displayed itself to the soldiers at the front. When before the need for human communication required human medians, the telephone used electricity as the median in which human communication was conducted. It was the median of communication that was transformed, not the human element of the communication.

All of this may seem relatively obvious to us from an outside observer position but never has this disclosure of the difference between the median of communication versus the human element of communication needed to be more addressed than in today's world. As the lightning speed of communication through social media becomes the absolute new standard, the idea that there is a human element at play within this median has ultimately become lost. Social media is now the status quo method of communication for all businesses and people across the globe. It is an addiction worth the lives of billions of people based upon the amount of time spent seeing to its fruition. The idea that there is a human element at the core of social media has become lost within the dependence on the median of communication itself. For social media is no different from that of telephone cable during the First World War. It is a mere median for communication between two people. It is not a substitute or an alternative to the human element at hand. No matter how we view the development of social media over the past decade as a median for communication, the one constant has always remained the same; the human element at the other end of that screen has remained just that.

Thirty-nine

A Version of the Truth

IT GOES FAR BEYOND imagination what the founding fathers of The United States of America could have predicted their creation turning into. In fact, the world of the 21st century is so far beyond recognizable to that first proposed in 1776, that to do so is a fool's errand and the purpose of any constitutional law academic. While there exist obvious universal human interpretations of what the American Revolution was meant to settle, the general consensus often clouds the reality of the age; an age of kings, land ownership through birthright, militias, freedoms through skin color and gender. The debates can rage forever about the ethics of it all, but for us today we are focused on one single article of the foundation of America. We want to focus on the idea that a version of the truth can be so powerful that it can simply take over any underlying natural truths more prevalent to the reality of the situation present.

In the history books sitting on every desk across the United States, the text reads very simply when discussing the revolutionary war; it was an action against tyranny and for freedom. The young nation ultimately beat the parent by using a cause of justice, desire for peaceful ideals and the virtuous path. Heroes were a plenty who would stand up for the common man and woman across the colonies with the intent to lift up thy brethren for the greater good of humankind. The founding fathers ushered in an age of righteous peace, in which all people have the opportunity to be whomever they want and practice the trials of life without duress. The wealthy bureaucrat and the poor farmer toiled against the rule of an oppressive monarch. The destruction of the birth right and the indoctrination of the opportunity of all people willing to work hard for their due. This belief was common when the revolutionary war was being fought and has stood the test of time. Popular sentiment today would have you believe that the truth is verbatim to that sold during the war itself. In reality, a mere version of the truth was enough to set in motion a three-hundred-year history we have all come to accept as the singular truth.

In order to dig deeper than the average high school textbook, we are going to need to label the state of affairs most often avoided by those lackluster specimens of historical science. One of the most prolific happenings pre-revolution was the growing distance between the English overlords, their army, the wealthy colonialists and every other American colonialist. Now the average person would have you believe that there were only two factions, nationalists and loyalists. The actual reality was that the divide was far greater within the colonies and it is easily demonstrated by the state of economics and laws at the time.

In some of the largest cities in the colonies during the 1770s, the wealth disparagement between the common nationalist and the wealthy nationalist was grave. Certain studies have gone to show that in Boston, for example, the top five percent of taxpayers owned almost half the taxable assets in the city. In many other major cities, the realities were very similar, with the wealthy retaining control over a majority of the productive assets. In the south, there was another additional class of individual; the slave. The majority of slaves were owned by the wealthy few, and the rest of the white male population was simply restricted to lower class with only the shackles removed from their existence as a symbol of status in the eyes of their wealthy employers.

Also, many of the laws placed into effect by the English crown had direct and immediate effect upon the lower classes of people. For example, the Quartering Act, which forced colonialist to allow British troops to reside in their abodes. Many of these measures ensured that the British were always treated with a sense of superiority over the colonial Americans. One of the biggest problems with laws like this was that it made even the middle-class colonialist a fourth, and sometimes even fifth, class party with only slaves being seen as inferior in states where this activity was legal. The anger towards upper classes within the colonies were initially not directed at the English rulers, for the English had a standing army and were a force to be reckoned with.

The mob mentality in the colonial states was a common occurrence after the conclusion of the war with the French and Indian nations in the west. Suppressing revolts was a normal conjuring by the wealthy aristocrats, whether they be English or colonialist. One of the most prevalent mob actions pre-revolutionary war was the War for Plunder, as it became known. Wealthy members of the colonialist population in Boston were subject to looting and pillaging of their estates. Andrew Oliver, a wealthy merchant, and Thomas Hutchinson, a wealthy aristocrat, were both victims of this plundering by the angry mob of lower class colonialists. The risk to the wealthy American asset holders was great, as fury was being garnered by the lower classes. The faction with the easiest target was the poorly protected colonial rich. To the rich colonialists, it appeared very quickly that this tenacity towards aggression apparent within the working classes needed to be redirected towards another source, for suppression of revolt became a futile approach.

One of the great names to come out of the revolution against England was the lower classman turned political influencer, Thomas Paine. By the time Paine had entered the picture, English laws and actions were continuously throwing kindling on an already burning fire of anger from both rich and poor colonialist, such as the Stamp Act, Townshend Taxes and the Boston Massacre. Paine had become, through his paper Common Sense, an outspoken political activist within the lower classes of the colonies. His papers spoke wildly about the powers that laborers are entitled within the political process, the rights of non-landowning men and the favorability of a centralized government. These views expressed a sophistication towards lower class ideals, ensuring that both the rich and the poor had a fair hand in the decision-making process within the new nation. To the eyes of men and women in the lower classes, Paine was one of them.

Paine though had his hand in many pots, and his associations and formal positions spoke a different story than what was demonstrated in Common Sense. His condemnation of the mob attack on the estate of James Wilson, who had made hard stances against the positions favorable to the lower class. James Wilson was an aggressive opportunist when it came to his material wealth, was of intense conservative viewpoints and held himself with the highest of aristocratic orders. Paine also was a close supporter of the wealthy Phillip Morris and was a staunch supporter of Morris's Bank of North America. While it was the impression that Paine was a firm hand in support of lower class rights that garnered his wide support base, it was his position also as a right hand of the wealthy nationalist status that ultimately lead to his success as a founding father.

In no way does Paine's story overshadow the enormity of the next founding father to have mixed loyalties during the revolutionary war. Thomas Jefferson has become known as the face of the revolutionary movement due to his material involvement in the actions that took place during the years before and after the revolution. Jefferson wrote the Declaration of Independence that was voted on and ratified as supreme law by the founding fathers. His well-known language stating, "All men are created equal," is a staple for the eyes and ears of people from all class systems across the world fighting against oppression and injustice. It is a strong collection of words for a strong statement at the time. Thomas Jefferson, in a paragraph within the Declaration, exposed and condemned the King of England for the transportation of slaves from Africa. His words were and to this day are a demonstration of the ideals that came out of the Revolutionary War and the Continental Congress. Jefferson was of the image of moral revulsion toward slavery, garnering him vast support within the northern colonies, even going so far as lending him assistance in his victory for president many years later. All of this was conducted with the fact that he personally was an exploiter of slave labor himself. In fact, he owned hundreds of slaves throughout the course of his life and all the way until the day he died. Eventually, the paragraph condemning slavery was removed from the final Declaration due to the sentiment of slave owning southerners involved in the Continental Congress.

For many, it is hard to imagine that the men we have come to know as proponents of change during a time of monarchs and political obsolescence of lower classes. The threat that the wealthy nationalists were experiencing during the years running up to the revolution were very real. The ability for lawyers, wealthy merchants and other leaders to create forums for people to meet and discuss grievances within public taverns and caucuses allowed for the dialogue of the revolution to take place. The financing of written work exposing the English King as the enemy of enemies' due to unfair laws helped turn the attention of the mob away from the wealthy exploiter down the street. The formal shaping of the Declaration of Independence with romantic words of inalienable rights ensured the common person was of the belief that their representatives were fighting for their political relevance. The hypocrisy of it all only goes to show that displaying a version of the truth, at the right time, in the right form, with the right audience and with the right resources can change the momentum of any course.

For the founding fathers, it was using already occurring anger to oust a monarch for a positive outcome. This could both suppress public rioting towards the wealthy colonialists and would also deepen the pockets of many of the already wealthy aristocratic opportunists in the bunch. A version of the truth can be a powerful tool that can destroy nations, inhibit power, transfer influence and ensure centuries of loyalty to half-hearted promises. In today's world, it is easy to get lost in the backstory of many of these characters, forgetting that through minor hypocrisy the common man and woman has eventually been able to obtain the inalienable rights promised so many years ago. The message in this passage must not be lost, that a version of the truth can garner a conclusion entirely different from that derived from the transparency of the whole truth or reality of the situation at large. A version of truth designed by the hands of the purveyor of a goal makes this goal that much easier to pitch, be purchased and consumed as a both a good and bad habit.

There is truthfully little left to be said to take this story into the 21st century. We are still living in a world founded by the men of the Continental Congress, even though the playing field has been leveled in an immense way since 1776. The average businessman or woman within the 21st century is afforded the same opportunities at specialized transparency that the founding fathers garnered all of those years ago. We see it in product commercials, public opinion, press releases, website banners, YouTube videos and mobile ads. A company who is able to express only a version of the truth, towards the benefit of their customer base, is far more competitive in that marketplace. A great salesperson is able to counter every negative idea with a version of positive inference. There is little that can be done to avoid this truth focusing, for it is a no longer a competitive advantage but rather a norm. If this custom is not adhered to by a young entrepreneur in the sales stage, the full transparency of the situation will crush any hope for success, for all offerings have a downside. The only answer to this practice is by building a product or service worth being transparent about, no matter the cost.

Lastly, if utilizing the version of truth norm ever leads an organization down the rabbit hole of insincerity and false truths, it is the immoral and illegal ramifications that will pounce on you deservingly. For if you ever cross the path into lying about your product or service offerings, the final clock will start to tick. There is a fine line between a version of the truth and a lie, for a version of the truth is grounded in a truth capable of being irrevocably defended. This defensible position will lead to a sale if exploited properly.

Forty

A Catalyst for Change

WHEN WE START A discussion on untouchable power and influence, very few instances in history can provide a pure enough version of the limitless influence garnered by the Roman Catholic Church during the Late Middle Ages. Each and every person living in Europe during this time was without question subject to the rule of law, status and sustenance of the church infrastructure. The rule of The Pope and his clergy was absolute, the power over kings, nobles, lords and even God himself. Every action was governed by the church, every motive questioned by the church and every person subject to the church. The power of The Pope wasn't brought into question on the matter of reach or jurisdiction, for God's reach was limitless and jurisdiction non-existent. But by all things governed by man, power will corrupt, and all character is derived by what men do with the power allotted them.

Any time when unanimous power must be taken into question, the path starts with an ability to question. Martin Luther was one such man, educated by some of the most prestigious schools in Germany at the time. His study was focused upon European theology, philosophy and the liberal arts. When time came to enter into a doctoral field to continue scholastic pursuits, theological study through monastic way of life called his name. Here, Luther could push the boundaries of his own intelligent and spiritual alignment to theology. Also, during these later scholastic years, Luther was involved in the inner workings of the Catholic legal process. Armed with the knowledge of the world of his age,

Martin Luther was prepared for a career of institutional Catholic servitude.

The Catholic Church at the end of the 15th century governed and ruled over every major aspect of society in Europe. Science, economics, military, politics and day-to-day life was all under the microscope of the church. The infrastructure present within the church was impressive and intimidating for all involved in its operation. Church Law was the method in which all courts operated, and excommunication by the church was the precursor to isolation and death. The church clergy debated the rules around running a continent on an almost daily occurrence, but the limits over the churches dominion was never brought into question. Also, the rule of The Pope was never questioned, but rather two sides would debate to influence the eventual rule of The Pope, for The Pope's words were parallel to the words of God himself.

Martin Luther was always a self-directed individual betraying his father's wishes for him to study law instead of theology at the later years of his education. The immeasurable size and complexity of the church at this time was not spared the strong personality of Martin Luther. One of the major factors that played into Luther's changing mentality towards the church as an institution was when Luther had discovered that a Dominican friar named Johann Tetzel was preaching some unfavorable practices to his congregation. Friar Tetzel preached the practice of purchasing, with coin or goods, the forgiveness of sin. Therefore, with enough money the wealthy could be spared from sin and guilt all while the poor would give their entire fortunes for the forgiveness of sins. To Luther, this was an abomination to the faith of Christendom. With this event, Martin Luther set about on a course of events that would change the course of history forever.

With motivation and an idea self-righteousness, Martin Luther drafted a list of 95 statements searching to make improvements to the Catholic institution as a whole. This draft of grievances was nailed onto the door of a chapel in Germany and was cemented into history as one of the great defying actions of humanity. The 95 went into areas of reformation that was prior to unheard of being brought into question. For example, some of the most well-known items of the list goes as such:

"Why does not the pope, whose wealth today is greater than the wealth of the richest Crassus, build the basilica of St. Peter with his own money rather than with the money of poor believers?"

"The pope cannot remit any guilt, except by declaring that it has been remitted by God and by assenting to God's remission; though, to be sure, he may grant remission in cases reserved to his judgment. If his right to grant remission in such cases were despised, the guilt would remain entirely unforgiven."

"Christians are to be taught that unless they have more than they need, they are bound to keep back what is necessary for their own families, and by no means to squander it on pardons."

"To think the papal pardons so great that they could absolve a man even if he had committed an impossible sin and violated the Mother of God — this is madness."

As one could imagine, the four statements above were enough to warrant an immense spectrum of repercussions harnessed by the church's influence and power. Martin Luther was accordingly subject to several trials by the church where all the statements were studied and debated. Martin Luther was eventually excommunicated and exiled from open practice within the Catholic Church, but his statements went on to become one of the most influential articles of conversation across all of Western Europe. Martin Luther was ordered to repudiate the statements made to achieve forgiveness in both the eyes of the church and ultimately the eyes of God. Luther made no retreat at the statements and continued to be a voice of revolution within the church.

One of the great accomplishments Martin Luther had on the history of the world was the breakup of the Catholic Church across Western Europe into sub sections of Christianity. No longer was the church as a single entity in control of the nations of Europe. Protestant reformation and nationalization played a heavy hand in the events over the next few centuries leading up into the modern world. Many believe that the great Renaissance of Europe was in large part due to the revolution inspired by Martin Luther that one fall day. Once a spark of enlightenment was birthed into the minds of Luther's fellow men and women, the raging fire of change swept through the church. Never again did the church and The Pope hold so much unanimous power over the lives of people.

Learning from the story of Martin Luther is one of the best ways to create a revolutionary movement worthy of the storybooks. Luther's progress is literally a step by step guide at how to achieve a legendary accomplishment, whether that be global reformation of idea, the launch of a great new product or the exposure of your niche service offering. There is no limit to what the following steps can garner in your life.

Preparation – Knowledge is power, study is your greatest weapon, practice and repetition is the key to perfection, opinion is somewhere in between ignorance and knowledge

Inspiration – Find your muse, be playful and mindful, embrace conflicting ideas, never stray from a challenging path

Motivation – Positivity supports action faster than negativity, a voice of reason is worse than a nail through the hand, idealism is the precursor to change, you were born into the same world as everyone else

Action – Ability is nothing without opportunity, showing up is half the battle, the first step is the hardest step, the world today was physically built by hands no different from your very own

Revolution – Great thought comes through great controversy, mediocrity viewed as original thought is the result of grand ignorance, stagnation packaged as change results in nothing but provide comfort to those dependent on the current allocation of power

Strength of Will – Any legendary thought will be criticized to the point of unreason by those with everything to lose, logic is the first item lost in the battle for survival, your courage is the greatest enemy to your enemy, capability aligned with practicality is the coup de grace to societal dormancy

Profit – *insert your own story here*

Bibliography

Arnold, James R. (2005). Marengo & Hohenlinden: Napoleon's Rise to Power: Pen & Sword.

Bachman, David. (1991). Bureaucracy, Economy, and Leadership in China: The Institutional Origins of the Great Leap Forward. New York: Cambridge University Press.

Baker, Chris. longlongtrail.co.uk. (2017). Milverton Associates. The Cambrai operations, 1917 (Battle of Cambrai). http://www.longlongtrail.co.uk/battles/battles-of-the-western-front-in-france-and-flanders/the-cambrai-operations-1917-battle-of-cambrai/.

Bawden, Charles R. (April 18, 2017). Genghis Khan. Encyclopaedia Britannica. https://www.britannica.com/biography/Genghis-Khan.

Biography.com Editors. (April 27, 2017). Genghis Khan Biography.com. A&E Television Networks. https://www.biography.com/people/genghis-khan-9308634.

biography.com. (2017). Julius Caesar Biography.com. https://www.biography.com/people/julius-caesar-9192504#synopsis.

Bos, Joan. madmonarchs.guusbeltman.nl. (July 4, 2012). J.N.W. Bos. Sado of Korea. http://madmonarchs.guusbeltman.nl/madmonarchs/sado/sado_bio.htm

Bressler, Richard (October 6, 2015). Frederick II: The Wonder of the World. Yardley, Pennsylvania: Westholme

Buchanan, John. (July, 1 1991). The Road to Guilford Courthouse: The American Revolution in the Carolinas: Wiley.

Dodge, Theodore Ayrault. (August 3, 2012). Hannibal: A History of the Art of War Among the Carthaginians and Romans Down to the Battle of Pydna, 168 B.C., With a Detailed Account of the Second Punic War: Tales End Press.

Eifler, Mark A. (2002). Gold Rush Capitalists: Greed and Growth in Sacramento. Albuquerque: University of New Mexico Press.

englishmonarchs.co.uk. (2005). Plantagenet. Henry II 1154-89. http://www.englishmonarchs.co.uk/plantagenet.htm.

englishmonarchs.co.uk. (2005). Plantagenet. Richard I the Lionheart. 1189-99. http://www.englishmonarchs.co.uk/plantagenet_2.htm.

Esdaile, Charles. (October 27, 2009). Napoleon's Wars: An International History: Penguin Books; First Edition.

Esther. Gods Word. Milton Keynes: Scripture Union, 2001. Print.

Ethier, Eric. (Feb. 23 2005). The Freeper Foxhole Remembers The Race to Messina (Jul-Aug 1943). American History Magazine.

eyewitnesstohistory. (2004). The Assassination of Julius Caesar, 44 BC, EyeWitness to History, www.eyewitnesstohistory.com/caesar2.htm.

eyewitnesstohistory.com. (2010). The Assassination of President William McKinley, 1901, EyeWitness to History. http://www.eyewitnesstohistory.com/mckinley.htm.

Fest, Joachim. (September 9, 2002). Speer: The Final Verdict, translated by Ewald Osers and Alexandra Dring: Harcourt; 1st US edition.

Frye, David G. (Spring 2007). Rome's Barbarian Mercenaries. Military History Quarterly. http://www.historynet/romes-barbarian-mercenaries.htm.

Gascoigne, Bamber. History of Sparta. HistoryWorld. From 2001, ongoing. The Spartan experience: from the 8th century BC. http://www.historyworld.net/wrldhis/PlainTextHistories.asp?ParagraphID=cer.

Glantz, David M. (October 1, 2011) Operation Barbarossa: Hitler's Invasion of Russia 1941: The History Press.

Goldsworthy, Adrian. historynet.com. (May 17, 2007). Julius Caesar's Triumph in Gaul. http://www.historynet.com/julius-caesars-triumph-in-gaul.htm.

Goodwin, Doris Kearns. (October 1, 1995). NO ORDINARY TIME: Franklin and Eleanor Roosevelt: The Home Front in World War II: Simon & Schuster; 1st edition.

Harrison, Kathryn. (October 28, 2014). Joan of Arc: A Life Transfigured: Doubleday.

Harrison, Mark. (March 22, 1993). The Soviet Defense Industry Complex in World War II. University of Warwick. Published in World War II and the Transformation of Business Systems, pp. 237-62. Edited by Jun Sakudo and Takao Shiba. Tokyo: University of Tokyo Press, 1994.

Herbermann, C., & Grupp, G. (1908). Constantine the Great. In The Catholic Encyclopedia. New York: Robert Appleton Company. Retrieved January 16, 2017 from New Advent: http://www.newadvent.org/cathen/04295c.htm.

Higgins, George A. (1985). Operational Tenets Of Generals Heinz Guderian And George S. Patton, Jr.

Hillerbrand, Hans J. (January 24, 2017). Encyclopaedia Britannica. Martin Luther. https://www.britannica.com/biography/Martin-Luther.

Hindley, Geoffrey. (March 25, 2004) A Brief History of the Crusades: Islam and Christianity in the Struggle for World Supremacy: Robinson Publishing

histclo.com. Origin. (September 1, 2012). German World War II Economics: Raw Materials--Oil. http://histclo.com/essay/war/ww2/eco/raw/oil/w2ero-ger.html

History.com Staff. (2009). history.com. Egyptian Pyramids. A+E Networks. http://www.history.com/topics/ancient-history/the-egyptian-pyramids

history.state.gov. Barbary Wars, 1801–1805 and 1815–1816. https://history.state.gov/milestones/1801-1829/barbary-wars.

Kladky, William P. mountvernon.org. Continental Army. http://www.mountvernon.org/digital-encyclopedia/article/continental-army/.

Korda, Michael. (May 6, 2008). Ike: An American Hero: Harper Perennial; Reprint edition.

livius.org. (1998 & 2017). Jona Lendering. Hannibal in the Alps. http://www.livius.org/articles/person/hannibal-3-barca/hannibal-in-the-alps/.

Luther, Martin. (March 14, 2013). Martin Luther's Ninety-Five Theses and Selected Sermons: Start Publishing LLC.

MacKay, James. (March 1, 1996). William Wallace: Brave Heart: Mainstream Publishing.

Mauer, Mauer, ed. (1979). The Battle of St. Mihiel. The US Air Service in World War I. Volume III. Washington DC: Office of Air Force History, Headquarters USAF. Stock Number 008-070-00385-6. Appendix A: Order of Battle, First Army, 12 September 1918.

McFall, Arthur J. (February 1998). First Crusade: People's Crusade. Military History Magazine.

Meyers, Jeffrey. (September 5, 2000). Edgar Allen Poe: His Life and Legacy: Cooper Square Press.

Miles, Gaile Phillips. typicallyspanish.com. (2014). Spanish War of Independence - The Motín de Aranjuez. http://www.typicallyspanish.com/news-spain/history/Spanish_War_of_Independence_-_The_Mot_n_de_Aranjuez.shtml.

militaryFactory.com. Content 2003-2017. Tank Mk IV Heavy Tank / Armored Fighting. http://www.militaryfactory.com/armor/detail.asp?armor_id=234.

Miller, Stephen, napoleon-series.org. (February 2005). King Joseph I's Government in Spain and its Empire. http://www.napoleon-series.org/research/government/spain/c_kingjoseph.html.

Minard, Charles Joseph. cartographia.wordpress.com. (June 2, 2008). Hannibal Crosses the Alps. https://cartographia.wordpress.com/2008/06/02/hannibal-crosses-the-alps/.

Mindel, Nissan. (07 Oct, 2007). Mordechai and Esther, Complete Story of Purim. Kehot Publication Society.

http://www.chabad.org/holidays/purim/article_cdo/aid/1348/jewish/
Mordechai-and-Esther.htm.

Moorehead Alan. (December 3, 2002). Prennial Classics Gallipoli: Harper
Prennial Modern Classics; Reprint edition.

Morris, Edmund. (November 2001). The Rise of Theodore Roosevelt:
Random House Trade Paperbacks; Reprint Edition.

Morris, Marc. (June 14, 2016). Great and Terrible King: Edward I and
the Forging of Britain: Pegasus Books.

napoleonistyka.atspace.com. (2001). "Napoleon's Strategy and Tactics" ,
http://napolun.com/mirror/napoleonistyka.atspace.com/Napoleon_tact
ics.htm#napoleonstrategy.

nobelprize.org. (19 Jun 2017). Nobel Media AB 2014. Web. George C.
Marshall - Biographical.
http://www.nobelprize.org/nobel_prizes/peace/laureates/1953/marsh
all-bio.html.

nps.gov. (February 26, 2015). T. R. the Rough Rider: Hero of the Spanish
American War. https://www.nps.gov/thrb/learn/historyculture/tr-rr-
spanamwar.htm.

Payne, Stanley G. (Jan 1, 1973). A History of Spain and Portugal:
University of Wisconson Press.

Poe, Edgar Allen. (February 17, 2013). The Raven: CreateSpace
Independent Publishing Platform.

Raphael, Ray. Zinn, Howard. (July 5, 2016). A People's History of the
American Revolution: How Common People Shaped the Fight for
Independence: The New Press.

Reston Jr., James. (May, 14, 2002). Warriors of God: Richard the
Lionheart and Saladin in the Third Crusade: Anchor.

Selin, Shannon. shannonselin.com. (2013-2017). Napoleon II: Napoleon's
son, the King of Rome. http://shannonselin.com/2014/02/napoleon-ii-
napoleons-son-king-rome/.

Smitha, Frank E. fsmitha.com. (2015). Rebellion against Spain in Latin
America. http://www.fsmitha.com/h3/h39-la.html.

spartacus-educational.com. (1997) (updated 2014). John Simkin. Erwin Rommel. http://spartacus-educational.com/GERrommel.htm.

Stevelinck, Ernest and Most, Kenneth S. (Spring 1985). The Accounting Historians Journal. Vol. 12, No. 1.

The Editors of Encyclopaedia Britannica. (June 15, 2017) Encyclopaedia Brtinnica, Inc. https://www.britannica.com/event/French-and-Indian-War.

The Editors of Encyclopaedia Britannica. (June 19, 2017). Sir William Wallace: Encyclopaedia Britannica. https://www.britannica.com/biography/William-Wallace.

Theobald, Ulrich. chinaknowledge.de. (October 16, 2011). Chinese History - The City-States of the Silk Road. http://www.chinaknowledge.de/History/Altera/citystates.html.

Tuchman, Barbara W. (July 22, 2009). The Guns of August: The Outbreak of World War I; Barbara W. Tuchman's Great War Series: Random House.

Victor Cunrui Xiong (2006). Emperor Yang of the Sui Dynasty: His Life, Times, and Legacy. SUNY Press.

Williamson, Allen. Biography of Joan of Arc. (2014). Joan of Arc Archive. http://joan-of-arc.org/joanofarc_biography.html.

Wright, Kevin W. bergencountyhistory.org. BARON VON STEUBEN. With Particulars Regarding His Jersey Estate. http://bergencountyhistory.org/Pages/gnsteuben.html.

wwiivehicles.com. (1999 to 2017). Aircraft Production & Tank Production. http://www.wwiivehicles.com/default.asp.